INFINITY'S ILLUSTRATED CLASSICS

Around the World in Eighty Days

& Five Weeks in a Balloon

JULES VERNE

Retold by W. Sequeira & A. D' Souza and Re-illustrated.

INFINITY BOOKS

AROUND THE WORLD IN EIGHTY DAYS

ISBN 81-7929-252-5

First Edition of 18 Titles 2001, Reprinted 2002, 2003, 2004 (Twice), 2005 (For export), 2006, 2007, 2008, 2010, 2011, 2012, 2013 & 2014 (Special Edition), 2015, 2016, 2017.

Published for:

ADARSH ENTERPRISES

4393/4 Tulsidas Street, Ansari Road,
Darya Ganj, New Delhi-110002
Phones: 23246131, 23246132. Fax: 011-23246130.
Email: adarshbooks@vsnl.com

Printed at : Saurabh Printers Pvt. Ltd.

CONTENTS

FOGG GETS A SERVANT

The house which Sheridan occupied in 1872, No.7, Saville Row, Burlington Gardens, was occupied by Phileas Fogg, a member of the Reforms Club in London. He was compared to Lord Byron because of the shape of his head. Fogg, though not a Londoner, was a Britisher. He never visited the Stock Exchange, Bank or any other office in the City Bank, or any office in the city. He did not own any ship, Was not on the Board of Directors anywhere, was not a lawyer, not a merchant, tradesman or farmer.

He was nothing else but a member of the Reforms Club, to which exclusive Club he had been recommended by Messrs. Baring Brothers. He was definitely a rich man but no one knew how he had acquired his fortune. He was not extravagant but was always ready to contribute for any worthy cause. He spoke very little but knew everything about any part of the world without ever having left London. He could always be seen at the Club where his only occupation was reading the papers and playing whist. He played whist not for winning but as a challenge because his winnings were kept aside for charity. He was a bachelor and had no relatives or friends.

He had one servant to look after him but he had all his meals at the Club. He was served in special china dishes and had his sherry, port or claret in special glasses. The ice he used had to be imported for him. He was very rigid and punctual in his habits. That same day he had dismissed his servant for giving him shaving water at 84 degrees F instead of 86 degrees F and was waiting for the new servant to come between 11 and 11.30.

At this moment his old servant James Foster knocked and ushered in the new servant, a thirty year old person." Your name is John and you are French?" asked Fogg. "Jean, if you please sir, Jean Passepartout. I am an honest person and to earn a living I have done tight-rope walking, street singing, vaulting, and also been a

Fogg meets Jean Passepartout.

fireman. I left France 5 years ago and I would now like to lead a quiet life so when I heard about you I applied." "You know my terms?" asked Fogg. "Yes, sir" was the reply.

"Well, you are employed from now, 11. 29 a.m, Wednesday, October 2nd, 1872." said Fogg and left the room for the club. Foster too went and Jean was alone.

JEAN EXAMINES THE HOUSE

Passepartout said to himself, “Oh !” my master has as much emotion as the wax figures in Madame Tussaud’s!” He judged his master to be 40 with a noble bearing, slightly stout, tall, a very cool person possessing very accurate habits.

Jean himself was a real Parisian, with a look of assurance and indifference. He had a chubby face, a warm complexion and a broad and muscular figure, and brown hair.

It was now 11.30 and he started to inspect the house. It was clean, well-kept and austere. His room was on the third floor and was provided with speaking tubes through which he could communicate with any room on the other floors. On the mantlepiece there was a card on which the whole day's routine was given. Tea and toast at 8.23, shaving water at 9.37 and hair dressing at 9.50 etc. Fogg's ward robe was tastefully chosen. Every coat, waistcoat and trousers had a number and were entered in a register which showed when they had to be taken out and worn. The same with his numerous pairs of shoes.

After examining the house in detail, Passepartout exclaimed, "This is exactly what I wanted and will suit me perfectly. We will get on very well together!"

DIAMONDS ARE TRUMPS

Fogg left home at 11.30 and, after taking 1151 strides, reached Reform Club. He went straight into the dining room, sat at his usual table and ordered his lunch of a side dish, fish, sauce, roast beef and a bit of cheese washed down with plenty of excellent tea. At 12.47 he went to the drawing room and read the Times till 3.45 and read the Standard till dinner time after which he had his dinner.

At 5.40 he entered the drawing room and took the Morning Chronicle and sat. After half an hour his friends and whist partners entered. They were Andrew Stuart, engineer, bankers John Sullivan and Samuel Fallentin, Thomas Flanagan the brewer and Gautier a governor of the Bank of England. All rich and respected men.

"How now, Ralph," said Flanagan, "what do you think of this bank robbery?" "Well," replied Stuart," the bank will lose the money." "I don't think so," Ralph said, "police inspectors have been sent all over the world including America and Europe to nab the thief." "But according to the Morning Chronicle, it was not a thief, but a gentleman who had stolen 55000 pounds from the Bank of England!" Fogg informed and bowing joined them.

When one of them asked how this amount could be stolen so easily, Ralph replied that at the time, the cashier was busy entering in the ledger. But, to make matters worse, the Bank of England trusts the public implicitly so they have no guards, gratings or old soldiers. The money is openly exposed.Once he had seen a curious incident. An ingot of gold weighing 7 or 8 pounds was handed from one to the next person in the Queue until, after all had examined it, it was returned to the cashier who had not looked up even once! But on September 29th when the cash was tallied in the evening, it was found that 55,000 pounds were missing. Then the police were alerted and sent all over with the announcement of a reward of 2000 pounds and 5 percent of the sum recovered.

On the day in question, a well-dressed

gentleman had been seen walking about near so a description of the man was obtained and despatched to detectives of all near by countries. It was discussed all over London whether the culprit would be caught or not. Even at the Reform Club they were arguing the matter. Andrew Stuart said, "The world is such a large place that he can hide anywhere and escape detection." Fogg replied, "It was large but is no longer so." "I agree with Mr. Fogg," said Ralph, "the world has become smaller. Compared to a hundred years ago, now one can easily travel over it in 3 months."

"I say, in eighty days." said Fogg." "Yes," said John Sullivan," the Morning Chronicle has tabulated the journey:

London to Suez via Mt. Cenis and Brindisi by rail and boat ....7 days

Suez to Bombay by boat ....13 days
Bombay to Calcutta by rail ....3 days
Calcutta to Hong Kong by boat
.........13 days
Hong Kong to Yokohama by boat
............6 days
Yokohama to San Francisco by boat
........22 days..
San Francisco to New York by rail
..........7 days
New York to London by boat and rail
...........9 days
TOTAL ....80 days

Stuart added, "Yes, 80 days. But taking into account rough weather, storms and wrecks etc." To this, Fogg replied, "Yes taking into account everything. 80 days!"

"In theory you are right, Fogg, but

practically," Stuart said, "I would like to see you do it. I will bet 4000 pounds that you cannot do it." In the end each of the partners bet 4000 pounds and Fogg put 20000 pounds. Fogg again said, "I have now wagered that I will travel around the world in 80 days or less, that is, in 1920 hours or 115200 minutes. Do you accept?" They all nodded.

"All right," said Fogg, "the train to Dover leaves at 8.45 this evening, I will catch it. Today is Wednesday, 2nd October, I shall be back in this drawing room of Reform Club on Saturday, the 21st December at 8.45 p.m. Here is my cheque for 20000 pounds. It was now 7 O'clock and when Fogg was asked if he wished to continue the game, he dealt the cards and said, "Diamonds are trumps, you begin, Mr. Stuart."

The bet.

THE JOURNEY BEGINS

At 7.25 Fogg left the club and returned home at 7.50. He went straight to his room summoned Passepartout who was surprised as this was not the time according to the regular schedule for him to return home.

When Jean went up, Fogg said, "We are going to start for Dover and Calais in ten minutes. We go around the world in 80 days." "Around the world?" said Passepartout,

"No trunks, replied Fogg,
"iust a travelling bag."

then we must hurry. Shall I pack the trunks?"

"No trunks," replied Fogg, "just a travelling bag. Put in 2 woollen shirts and 3 pairs of stockings and the same for yourself. Get my raincoat and rug. Keep some sturdy boots also."

Then Passepartout made all the preparations and got ready to see his beloved Paris again. At 8 o'clock they were ready to move. Fogg took the bag from Jean and stuffed bundles of bank notes in it and gave it to Jean saying, "Be careful with it; it contains 20000 pounds." They came down, locked the front door,took a cab, reached Charing Cross Station at 8.20, bought two first class tickets and proceeded to the platform where Fogg saw his five friends standing.

"Friends, I am going. I will get my visa

Fogg meets his five friends.

stamped enroute as proof. On Saturday, December 21st at 8.45 p.m, I will meet you. Goodbye till then!" Fogg told them. They got in the train and at 8.45 it started. Suddenly Passepartout said, "Oh! God! I forgot to shut the gas in my room!"

"Well, young man, it will burn at your expense!" said Fogg.

WAGERS FOR AND AGAINST

This wager was discussed in the Club for and against Fogg's venture. The Times, Evening Chronicle and many papers were against Fogg. The Daily Telegraph was in his favour. Some called him a madman and some blamed his friends.

A long article was published by the Royal Geographical Society that they could encounter many difficulties like weather, accidents, storms, derailment, dacoits etc. and be delayed. The public also started betting for and against him.

The Chief of Polce received a message: "Suez. Rowan, Chief of Police, Scotland Yard, London. Am shadowing Phileas Fogg, bank robber. Send warrant for arrest to Bombay. Detective Fix." From honourable gentleman he had become bank thief!

MR. FIX TRIES TO FIX FOGG

The Mongolia was due to arrive at Suez at 11 a.m. She was a very fast boat. On the wharf were two men waiting for the liner. One was the British Consul, Stephenson and the other was a small thin man. His name was Fix, an English detective sent to watch the port for the bank thief. He was getting quite impatient.

The consul said to Fix," I don't know how

On the wharf were two men waiting for the liner.

you will spot your man among so many passengers. Fix replied, "We have to scent them out. This requires flair." "I wish you luck, Mr. Fix." said the consul.

A shrill whistle was heard and there was commotion on the wharf with porters and fellahs rushing to meet the Mongolia. Soon the Mongolia entered the harbour and the passengers disembarked. One of the passengers approached Fix and asked him the way to the British consulate. Fix took the passport and when he scanned it, he was seized with emotion.

"This is not yours?" he asked. "No, it is my master's." was the reply "he will have to go himself to the consulate." said Fix. Alright, I will fetch him." Saying this, the passenger bowed and went back to the liner.

NEITHER GAINED NOR LOST TIME

The detective then rushed to the consul's office and told him about Fogg's arrival and that he suspected him to be the bank robber. "I don't think he will come here," said the consul, "a thief never leaves his traces behind him." Fix replied, "He is a very clever thief and I am sure he will come." "If his passport is right, I cannot refuse to visa it." the consul said. Just then there was a knock on the door and Fogg entered to get his passport visaed. “You are Mr.Fogg?” asked the consul.” “Yes.” And this man is your servant?” “Yes, a Frenchman called Passepartout.” replied Fogg. The consul then visaed the passport. Mr. Fogg then returned to the wharf, took a boat and returned to the Mongolia and wrote in his diary :

“Left London Wednesday, October 2nd, 8.45 p.m

“Arrived Paris, Thursday, October 3rd, 7.20 a.m

“Left Paris, Thursday, 8.40 a.m

“Arrived Turin by Mont-Cenis, Friday, October, 4th, 6.35 a.m

“Left Turin, friday, 7.20 a.m

“Arrived Brindisi, Saturday, October 5th, 4 p.m.

The consul then visaed the passport.

"Sailed on the Mongolia, Saturday 5 p.m
"Arrived Suez, Wednesday, October 9th,11 a.m
"Total hours spent, 158 1/2 or days, 6 1/2"

Fogg kept this record to see if he gained or lost time during his journey. He had not lost any time so far.

Then he ordered lunch since he was not interested in sight-seeing.

FIX FOLLOWS FOGG

Fix met Passepartout on the wharf and asked him," Is your passport visaed?" "Yes,." said Jean," but we are travelling so fast that I do not have a chance to see Paris as all I could see was through rushing cab windows. "Are you in such a hurry?" asked Fix." "Yes," we left London with only one bag. Now I must purchase some socks and shirts." Fix accompanied Jean to the market. "I must

"Is your master rich?" asked Fix.

not miss the boat." said Passepartout. Fix told him that it was only 12 o'clock and there was plenty of time for the boat. Passepartout looked at his watch and said," "12 o'clock! It is 8 minutes to 10 by my watch which is a family heirloom! It is a perfect watch." Fix told him it is London time which is 2 hours behind Suez time and that he should reset his watch in each country. "Never!" said Jean. "Is your master rich?" asked Fix. Jean replied, "Yes. He is carrying a lot of money in new notes and spending lavishly. He has promised the captain of the Mongolia a good reward to get us to Bombay before time."

This statement strenghtened Fix's suspicions further that Fogg was the thief. Passepartout proceeded to the market while Fix went to meet the consul. He narrated to him all that Jean had told him and said, "I will send a message to London Police to

Passepartout proceeded to the market.

despatch a warrant for the arrest of Fogg to Bombay and I will sail on the Mongolia to Bombay and arrest him on British soil." saying this, he sent the telegram and boarded the Mongolia.

The ship was soon speeding over the Red Sea for Bombay.

THEY REACH THE COAST OF INDIA

The distance between Suez and Aden is 1310 miles and takes 138 hours to cross but the Mongolia was going at so fast a speed that she would reach well before time. Most of the passengers were going either to Bombay or Calcutta. They consisted of Government officers, army men and businessmen. There were a few ladies. The sea sometimes was rough but inspite of this, the Mongolia raced ahead Fog did not show any apprehension but was very calm. He ate well and also found partners for games of whist. As for Passepartout, he was enjoying the voyage.

One day he met Fix on the deck and they started to talk. Jean asked him, “Where are you going?” “To India.” replied Fix. Passepartout remarked that India must be a very curious country.

“Very curious,” replied Fix, “temples, minarettes, dancing girls, fakirs, pagodas, tigers, snakes. I hope you will have time to do sight-seeing.” Jean replied, “I hope so. I am tired of jumping from train to steamer to train all the time.” The steamer was making good time. On the 13th they sighted Mocha with it's ruined walls,date palms and coffee fields. The next night they crossed the Straits of Ba-el-Mandeb and next day she stopped at Steamer Point to take coal.

Passepartout meets Fix on the deck.

Mr. Fogg and Jean went ashore and had the passport visaed and returned to the ship. At 6 o'clock the Mongolia was racing towards Bombay. The next day, Sunday, Oct. 20th, the Indian coast line was seen. The pilot came aboard and steered the ship past Salcette, Colaba, Elephanta and Bucher and at 4 O'clock she berthed along the quays of Bombay.

The Mongolia, due on the 22nd, arrived on the 20th. Two days in advance.

JEAN'S ESCAPE FROM THE PRIESTS

India is a vast country,one million four hundred thousand square miles in area. But British India is not more than seven hundred thousand square miles. In the early days people travelled on foot, horses, carts, wheel-barrows, palanquins etc. Now steam boats and trains arc thc modc of travel.

The passengers of the Mongolia landed at 4.30 and the train to Calcutta was at 8 p.m.

Phileas Fogg got off and went straight to the passport office for the visa and went to the railway station from there.Before this, he entered a restaurant for dinner and ordered rabbit stew which he found tasted bad so he called the manager and asked, "Did this rabbit mew when killed?" The manager replied, "Mew, my Lord? I swear......" "Don't swear, cats were once sacred in India!" and he continued his meal.

During this time, Fix left the ship and went to the Bombay Police HQ and asked about the warrant. He was told that no warrant had arrived. He then requested the Chief to issue the warrant which was refused. He thought that Fogg would stay a few days at Bombay meanwhile the warrant would arrive from London.

Passepartout left the ship and, after buying a few shirts and socks, was going about watching the streets crowded with Parsees, Banias, Sindhis and Armenians. It was a Parsee festival so he came across processions with dancers and loud music. After he had seen this, he was passing the Pagoda on Malabar Hill which he entered to see inside. He did not know that there are some religious places where Christains are forbidden to enter and the Government is very strict about this rule. Suddenly the priests caught hold of him and started beating him, pulling off his shoes and socks. As he was a very strong and agile man, he hit one priest to the ground and escaped.

At 7.55 he reached the station without hat or shoes or the parcel of purchases and told Fogg of his experience.Phileas heard him and warned him to be careful the next time. Fix, who saw them getting into the

Outside the temple.

train had overheard the story and he decided not to board the train.He said, "An offence has been committed on Indian soil. Now I have got them in my hands!"

Just then the engine whistled loudly and the train moved off.

ON THE BACK OF AN ELEPHANT

Passepartout and Fogg were in a compartment with Sir Francis Comarty, aged 50, who was in the army and had gone to India young, and visited his country England, once in a while.

Mr. Fogg had told all about his wager to the brigadier general who thought it was only a silly whim. In one hour the train had crossed Salcette, Kalyan, and entered the line to Khandala and Poona and came to Panvel station. Now they had reached the Western Ghats. The brigadier told Fogg that he may have to face some problem regarding Jean's trouble in the Pagoda since the Government was very strict about such things. "Yes," said Fogg, "if he was caught he would have been jailed and then gone back to England but that would not have delayed me." During the night thay crossed the ghats and Nasik and entered a thick forest. In the morning they passed Malegaon and entered the Nizam's territory and crossed Ellora and Aurangabad.

Upto now, Passepartout had thought that their journey would end at Bombay and now he was thrilled at whizzing across India that he began to get worried at the slightest delay and whenever the train stopped. The next day at 8 o'clock, the brigadier asked Jean the time and when Jean said it was 3 a.m, Sir Francis told him to correct the watch as it was showing London time which Passepartout refused to do as he had refused Fix.

At 8 a.m the train stopped a little after Rothal and the guard went along the carriages announcing, "All change! All change!" Fogg and Sir Francis were surprised and Passepartout got down to see what was the matter and came back and said, "Sir, this is the end of the railway!" The guard explained, "We are at Kholby hamlet, the line ends here as the rails have not yet been laid." "But the papers said the line was completed." "Well, sir, the papers are wrong. There is no line upto Allahabad."

Fogg suggested to Sir Francis that they find some other transport upto Allhabad and

The end of the railway.

went out of the station but all transport had already been taken by other passengers. Phileas said he would walk. Just then Jean came and said, "I have found transport, sir. An elephant belonging to an Indian living nearby." Five minutes later the three went to a hut of an Indian with a paddock where a huge elephant was kept. It was reared, not a beast of burden but as a fighter by feeding him on sugar and butter for 3 months.

Elephants are not cheap in India and when Fogg asked him to give it on hire,the Indian refused. Fogg offered upto 40 pounds an hour yet it was refused so Fogg offered to buy the elephant for 1000 pounds. Still the man refused. Fogg was desperately in need so, after bargaining, the Indian agreed for two thousand pounds.

Then they searched for a guide and found

a nice young Parsee who was also an expert mahout. Phileas paid the owner and the guide got the elephant's saddles ready. Mr. Fogg offered to take Sir Francis with them who accepted the offer.

Then they bought all provisions for the trip and got on the elephant's back. At nine o'clock they departed from the town and proceeded by a short cut into a thick forest of fan-palms.

The elephant ride through the forest.

THE SUTTEE

The guide knew of a short cut so they followed it. Though Fogg and Sir Francis felt very uncomfortable on the elephant's back, they did not complain. Jean too was very uncomfortable but kept on joking and feeding sugar to the elephant whose name was Kiouni. After two hours they stopped for rest, and had breakfast. At noon they resumed their journey.

This was the territory of some fierce tribes and they even passed some but kept at a safe distance. The group crossed the Vindhya Range at 8 p.m and camped for the night at the rest house. They had covered 25 miles and had 25 more to reach Allahabad. After supper, they slept.

At 6 a.m, they started again hoping to reach Allahabad by evening. By noon the party reached near a small town called Kallinger and by two, they entered a thick forest. They heard some voices and sound of musical instruments. The Parsee jumped down and tied the elephant to a tree well-hidden. He said, "It is a group of Brahmins coming. We must hide. Don't get down till they pass." The procession came in sight soon.

First came the priests in long robes surrounded by men and women and children

She had on a lot of jewellery.

singing a dirge and beating cymbals and drums. Then came a statue on a car. It had 4 arms, a body with tangled hair, lolling tongue and a garland of skulls. Sir Francis said, "It is the goddess of death, Kali." Next came the Brahmins leading a young and very fair woman who could hardly stand. She had on a lot of jewellery. She was followed by armed guards carrying a dead body on a palanquin. It was the body of an old Rajah.

Sir Francis sadly said, "A Suttee." Phileas Fogg asked what a Suttee was and Sir Francis told him it is a human sacrifice and the woman would be burned along with her dead husband at dawn the next day. The British government had put down the practice but in some remote areas it was still practised.

He said, "This sacrifice is not a voluntary one but she has been drugged. She will be taken to the Pagoda of Pillagi and burnt tomorrow at dawn."

Since the procession had passed by now, the guide made ready to go when Fogg stopped him and said, "How about rescuing this woman? I have still 12 hours saved." "By Jove!," said the Brigadier, "you are a brave man." "Occasionally, when I have the time." said Fogg.

THE DEAD RAJAH RETURNS

Sir Francis and Passepartout both were ready to support Fogg in his bold scheme to rescue the young lady. Now they wondered how the guide would feel, but when they asked him he said, "Sir, I am a Parsee. I am with you in this scheme but it is too dangerous." Then he told them that the lovely lady was the daughter af a rich Parsee merchant of Bombay who had been married to the old Rajah. Her name was Aouda and had been educated in England.

Half an hour later they stopped near the Pagoda of Pillagi where the funeral party was. They thought they could rescue her at night when the guards were sleeping after bhang.They slowly crawled to the banks of the stream where the body of the Rajah was lying on the pyre. Then they went towards the pagoda. There was a multitude of people sleeping outside and the temple was guarded by armed and alert guards making it impossible to enter. They went to the back of the temple which was unguarded and tried to loosen the bricks of the wall and enter. While they were doing this, the guards heard the sound and gave the alarm; so they had to beat a hasty retreat. They were deeply disappointed. Sir Francis and the guide suggested that they should go

The Temple guard.

They tried to loosen the bricks of the wall.

away now but Fogg said, "Wait a bit. We may get a chance in daylight."

Passepartout made a plan of his own. He slowly slipped down the tree and waited. The night ended and there was a loud sound of singing and music. The doors of the pagoda opened and the woman was being brought out held tightly by two priests. It was clear that she was unwilling and the effects of the drug had worn off. She was put on the pyre with the body of the Rajah beside her and the pyre was lit.

Fogg and his companions followed them at a distance. Fogg was rushing towards the pyre but was held back by the guide and Sir Francis.

Suddenly there were loud shouts as a weird scene took shape at the pyre. The dead Rajah seemed to take up his wife in his arms

The dead Rajah took up his wife in his arms.

and jump down from the flames. He moved to where Mr. Fogg and his companions were hiding and said, "Come on.Let's be off!"

It was no other than Passepartout who had carried out this brave deed! Immediately the four dashed away in the jungle. There were shouts and a few shots but the rescue party had got away beyond reach of arrows or bullets.

FOGG MAKES AN OFFER TO AONDA

The abduction had succeeded. They were all happily congratulating Passepartout on his brave action. The young lady was still reposing. They now were making rapid progress through the forest. Sir Francis expressed his fear that if the lady whose name was Aouda remained in India these fanatics would surely find her and kill her; they reached Allahabad at 10 o'clock. They went straight to the station and Passepartout

Ending the elephant ride.

Fogg offers to take her to Hong Kong.

was sent to the market to buy clothes and a shawl and toiletries for Aouda who was beginning to recover from the effects of the drug. Just before the train was leaving, Mr. Fogg called the guide, paid him his exact wage and astounded him by presenting him with Kiouni, the elephant. Aouda had by this time recovered fully and thanked her deliverers profusely, but still showd her fear of discovery by those ruffians. Phileas Fogg offered to take her to Hong Kong and leave her with her relative there. When the train reached Benaras, Sir Francis got off to join his battalion. The train at last reached Calcutta at seven o'clock in the morning.

FOGG PAYS THE FINE

Phileas Fogg had planned to go to the Hong Kong boat direct from the station to settle Aouda comfortably but as they got off the train, a policeman met them and enquired, "Mr. Phileas Fogg?"

"Yes, that's my name." replied Fogg.

"Is this man your servant?"

"Yes."

"Both of you please follow me." Said the

He asked them both to follow him.

man. "May the young lady come with us?" asked Fogg to which the policeman replied, "Yes. In a 'palki ghari'." They went, passing through the Indian locality of small huts and the European locality of neat houses with gardens. They reached the Court where the man took them to a room and told them that the judge would arrive at 8.30. Passepartout was very worried that they would miss the boat and his master would lose the wager for a small mistake of his. At half past eight the judge arrived and they were taken before him. "The first case." said Judge Obadiah. The clerk called out, "Phileas and Passepartout." The judge said, "Prisoners at the bar, the police have been looking for you on all the trains from Bombay for the last two days." "But what is our crime?" Asked Passepartout. "That you will be told. Bring in the plaintiffs." called the judge. At his

They were taken before the Judge.

order, three priests were ushered in. Passepartuot muttered, “These are the scoundrels who tried to burn the young lady!” The three stood in front of the judge and the clerk read out the charge that Fogg and his servant had been accused of violating a religious place of the Hindus. The judge asked Fogg, “You have heard the accusation. Do you plead guilty or not guilty?” “Guilty, but ask them whether or not they were trying to burn the young lady before the Pagoda of Viragi.” said Fogg. The priests were astounded and said they knew nothing of Viragi but they were referring to the sacrilege committed by them in Bombay and they held aloft Passepartout’s shoes to prove it. The mischief had been played by Fix who had instigated the priests to file a case. He was also sitting hidden in a corner of the court.

Then the judge passed sentence saying, "The prisoner, Passepartout, for having desecrated a Hindu religious place, which crime the British Government takes a very serious view of, is fined 300 Pounds and 15 days in jail. The prisoner, Mr. Fogg, who has had no direct part in the offence, is fined 150 Pounds and 8 days in prison. But I am prepared to grant bail as both are strangers. The amount of bail will be one thousand Pounds each." Fogg reached in his bag and took out bank notes for two thousand Pounds and handed them to the clerk. Then the three of them walked out of the court. Fogg engaged a carriage and straight-away drove to the quay where the ship Rangoon was anchored. It was now eleven o'clock. The detective stamped his foot in rage and frustration when he saw them get into a boat and put off for the Rangoon and he thought,

Fogg paid the bail.

"Two thousand Pounds gone! None more wasteful than a thief! I will shadow him to the end of the world if I must." Fogg had already spent more than five thousand Pounds since leaving London and the percentage of the sum recovered, assigned as a reward for the detectives, was growing less day by day.

THE DETECTIVE IS DISAPPOINTED

The cabins in the Rangoon were not as well furnished as those on the Mongolia. During the voyage, Aouda tried to show her gratitude to Mr. Fogg in many ways but it had no effect on him. He behaved always in a very distant, cold and gentlemanly way towards her. Aouda was quite puzzled by this behaviour but Passepartout explained all about his master's character and all about the wager to her which was taking them around the world in eighty days. As for Aouda, she belonged to a rich Parsee businessman's family. Sir Jejeebhoy, a very rich Parsee merchant of Bombay was her relative and the gentleman Jejeeh by name, was his cousin with whom she had planned to stay in Hong Kong. She was worried whether he would keep and protect her but Fogg said not to worry and that all would be well. The voyage was going very smoothly and they sailed past the Andamans towards the Strait of Malacca to the China Sea. Meanwhile Fix was keeping himself out of sight on board. So his hopes were pinned on their stay at Hong Kong as the halt at Singapore was too short. He hoped to receive the arrest warrant on reaching Hong Kong so that he could arrest him and hand him over to the police as Hong Kong was still under the British Government. Should everything fail, he decided to tell Passepartout all about the theft and make him see what a thief his master was. He also wondered who the woman was and whether she had eloped with Fogg. This would be to his advantage as he could inform the Hong Kong police about this and put him in difficulty. But he must do so before they reached Hong Kong. He could do this by telegraphing them from Singapore. So he decided to accost Passepartout as if by chance and get some information from him. So he waited one day on deck and when he saw Passepartout he pretended to be surprised and said, "What you on board!" "Well Mr. Fix you are here. I thought I had left you at Bombay. Are you also going around the world?" said Passepartout." Oh no," replied Fix, "I intend to stay at Hong Kong for a few days. By the way, how is your master?" "He's

"What you on board!"

fine and we have not lost a single day. We have a young lady also with us." said Passepartout. Then Passepartout told him all about himself. About the incident in the Pagoda at Bombay. The purchase of the elephant for two thousand pounds. The rescue of the lady from Sutee and the conviction and bail of two thousand Pounds by Judge Obadiah. "But are you going to take the lady to London?" "No, she will be left with her reative at Hong Kong." Hearing this, the detective was very disappointed.

AOUDA TRIES TO BEWITCH FOGG

Passepartout and Fix met frequently on the deck. Now Passepartout began to wonder whether it was coincidence or design that Fix seemed to be with them wherever they went. Suez, Bombay and Hong Kong always on the same ships and trains with them. Now Passepartout started suspecting him of some other motives. He also felt that Fix would follow them also from Hong Kong and on the same boat. Yet it never occured to him that Fix was following his master thinking him a thief. Then he decided that Fix must be an agent of the other people in London who had made the wager to see whether Fogg would actually travel around the world. After passing the Straits of Malacca on the 30th October the Rangoon reached Singapore at 4 o'clock on the morning the next day to take on a supply of coal.She had reached twelve hours in advance.

Fogg went ashore with Aouda for a walk, stealthily followed by Fix while Passepartout went to make some purchases. After a two hour drive through the groves of palm trees, clove trees, the jungles full of apes and the squat houses surrounded by fruit gardens, they returned to the ship at ten o'clock where they found Passepartout waiting for them with a lot of luscious mangos.

At eleven, the ship weighed anchor and sailed. Fogg calculated that it should not take them more than six days to reach Hong Kong to catch the boat to Yokohama from Hong Kong on 6th November. Now the Rangoon was fully loaded with the coal as well as a lot of Hindu, Ceylonese, Chinese, Malay and Portuguese passengers who had embarked at Singapore. The sea also got rough at times making many of the passengers ill. Thus there was a little loss of time. Though Fogg was not worried about this, Passepartout was.

One day Fix said to Passepartout, "You seem to be in a great hurry to get to Hong Kong." "Yes," replied Passepartout. "You feel that Mr. Fogg is anxious to catch the ship from there to Yokohama?" "Yes'" replied Passepartout. "You really believe in this mysterious journey across the world?" "Yes," said Passepartout, "don't you?" "No, I don't." "You sly dog!" exclaimed Passepartout.

Then he asked Fix, "Will we leave you behind at Hong Kong?" "Well," said Fix,"I can't say. It's just possible that I may.........."

"Ah," interrupted Passepartout, "it would be nice to have you with us. Surely you say you are an agent of the shipping Company so you cannot stop on the way. Bombay was your destination, now you are almost in China, America is not far away and it is only one step away from Europe."

Fix returned to his cabin in a worried state of mind. He was wondering whether Passepartout had guessed that he was a detective and whether he had told his master. Then he decided that, if he could not arrest Fogg at Hong Kong, he would tell Passepartout everything.

Now Passepartout was noticing the many ways Aouda was trying to attract his master but that his master was immune to all her charms and remained aloof and cold towards her and he came to the conclusion that Fogg, though he was capable of heroism, he was not capable of love!

FOGG MAKES AN OFFER TO AOUDA

Now the weather became rough and on the 3rd and 4th November a gale started which lashed the waves with fury which reduced the speed of the ship considerably so it was estimated that she would reach Hong Kong 20 hours or more behind time. Though this may make him lose his connection at Hong Kong, Fogg was not perturbed but kept calm. But Passepartout and Aouda were very worried.

The gale lashed the waves with fury.

Fix was very happy as this would force Fogg to stay a few days at Hong Kong which would help Fix to nab him on receiving the warrant of arrest.

At last, during 4th November the storm abated and the wind shifted so the ship picked up speed and on the 6th they sighted

Hong Kong and the pilot stepped on board at 6 o'clock. Passepartout was so anxious but he did not dare to ask the pilot if the ship to Yokohama had sailed. But Fogg quietly asked him and the pilot told him that it was delayed due to some engine trouble and would sail only the next morning. At one o'clock the passengers could disembark.

Of course, they were one day late but the passage from Hong Kong to Yokohama would be very smooth and though it would last 22 days they would be able to make up the lost time.So Fogg was very calm.

On leaving the ship, Fogg took Aouda and kept her in a good hotel and went to find her relative, the merchant Jejeebhoy. At the Stock Exchange, he was told by one broker that Jejeebhoy had left Hong Kong and was now settled in Europe, in Holland. Phileas Fogg returned to the hotel and informed Aouda accordingly.

"What am I to do?" said Aouda "Very simple," he replied, "come to Europe with us." He then told Passepartout to go to the ship Carnatic and book three cabins to Yokohama. Passepartout was very happy that Aouda would accompanying them.

Aouda agrees to come to Europe.

PASSEPARTOUT IS DRUGGED

Hong Kong is a British dominion situated on the mouth of the Canton River. The inhabitants are mostly Chinese with some Europeans, Indians and Japanese. Passepartout went to book the cabins for the three of them. On the way he met Fix and went up to him and said, "Well Mr. Fix, have you decided to come to America with us? I am going to the Harbour to book our cabins on the Carnatic, come with me."

Fix, who was cursing his luck as the warrant had not yet arrived, agreed. When they reached the booking office, the clerk informed them that the repairs to the ship were completed and she would sail the same evening at eight.

Passepartout was very happy and said he would go and inform his master. But Fix saw a chance in this to delay Fogg's departure. He took Passepartout to one of the liquor and opium dens on the street and plied him with more and more liquor till Passepartout was quite drunk.

Then he told Passepartout that he was in reality a detective and his job was to arrest Fogg who had stolen a sum of fiftyfive thousand pounds in London from the Bank of England. If Passepartout helped him he would give five hundred pounds from the

He took Passepartout to a opium den.

two thousand pounds declared as reward. Passepartout was astounded and very angry, "What? you dare to accuse my master who is the most honourable man in the world of being a thief?"

"Then I will have to arrest you as an accomplice." said Fix. Passepartout buried his head in his hands. He could not imagine his master, a brave and chivalrous man who had risked his life to save Aouda to be a thief. "What do you want me to do?" he asked. "To delay his departure from Hong Kong till I receive the warrant of arrest." Passepartout said, "Never," and tried to rise, "even if you share the reward with me!"

Then Fix, very stealthily put some opium in Passepartout's drink and said, " Well, let's finish our drinks." As soon as Passepartout had gulped down the drugged drink, he fell

He fell unconscious.

unconscious and Fix quietly left the den feeling pleased as now he was sure that Fogg would not come to know of the change in the ship's sailing time and would miss the ship. Then Fix paid the bill and quietly left the tavern.

FOGG FINDS A BOAT

All this time Phileas Fogg and Aouda were strolling in the British quarter and when they returned to the hotel at night and enquired about Passepartout, they were told that he had not yet returned. In the morning too, he had not returned and as it was time to go to the harbour, Fogg ordered a cab and they left. When they reached they were told that the ship Carnatic had left the previous evening. Then Fix approached them and said, "Sir, were you not a passenger on board the Rangoon with me?" "Yes," said Fogg. Fix asked, "But is your servant not with you?" "No." "He may have sailed without you."said Fix, "were you not planning to go on that ship?" " Yes we were," replied Fogg "but now the next sailing is after one week" said Fix feeling very pleased.

He was shocked when Fogg said, "But there are lots of other ships besides the Carnatic." Saying this, Fogg walked off with Aouda. Fix followed them.

After three hours of searching the harbour for a ship, a sailor approached them and said, "Are you looking for a boat?" "Yes," said Fogg, "have you got one?" "Yes, your honour, a pilot boat No. 43." replied the sailor. "Will you take me to Yokohama?" asked Fogg, "I have missed the Carnatic and must reach

"Are you looking for a boat?"

Yokohama by the 14th to take the boat for San Francisco. I will pay you a hundred pounds a day and a bonus of two hundred if you get us there in time."

The pilot replied, "I cannot endanger my boat or crew by trying to reach Yokohama at this time of the year but I will take you to Shanghai which we can reach in four days. The Carnatic actually starts from Shanghai; Yokohama and Nagasaki are only ports of call. The Carnatic leaves Yokohama on the 11th at 7 o'clock. Give me one hour to buy provisions and we will start." "Done, are you the skipper?" "Yes, I am, my name is John Bunsby."

Fogg gave him 200 pounds as advance and was returning to the hotel to get his luggage when Fix requested him to take him also to which Fogg graciously agreed.

He introduced himself as John Bunsby.

At three o'clock exactly the Tankadere was ready to sail. There were still no signs of Passepartout so Fogg reported the matter to the police station and the French Embassy, proceeded to the hotel, picked up their luggage and boarded the Tankadere.

Bunsby showed them to their cabin apologising that it was not luxurious enough. Fix had already embarked before them. At ten minutes past three the Tankadere sailed with a fair wind.

A CANNON SHOT RENTS THE AIR

The Tankadere was making very good time as the winds and currents were very favourable. Fix had decided to go to America and get an extradition order and arrest Fogg. He was admiring the intelligence of the so-called bank robber who, he thought was planning to escape to America by a round-about route and enjoy the money he had stolen. One day he approached Fogg and offered to pay his share of the fare which

Fogg flatly refused to accept; by that evening they had covered more than a hundred miles. Since the wind was favourable and they were going fast, they were confident of reaching Shanghai in time.

At daybreak the wind started blowing harder and the skipper told Fogg that they were expecting a typhoon but it would blow from the south and this would increase their speed.Bunsby then made all arrangements to deal with the typhoon by furling all sails, taking in the boom and battening down the hatches. The storm struck at at eight o'clock that evening. It was so severe that the ship was lifted like a feather and sped on her way at full speed.

At nightfall the gale increased in fury and by noon the wind decreased and Bunsby declared that they were hardly a hundred miles from Shanghai which they would reach that day inspite of losing a few hours due to the changes in the direction of the storm at times.

All the passengers were nervous as they had to reach in time to catch the American liner .

The wind had by now slackened considerably and at seven o'clock they were three miles from Shanghai harbour when they saw the American ship sailing out of the harbour. "Curse it!" exclaimed Bunsby who felt the bonus of two hundred pounds slipping away.

Fogg then told him to put the flag at half mast, being the distress signal and to fire the cannon to attract her attention. "Fire off." said Phileas Fogg. The blast of the cannon rent the air!

They saw the American ship sailing out.

PASSEPARTOUT BADLY DISAPPOINTED

Meanwhile the Carnatic had sailed out of Hong Kong on November 7th at 6.30 p.m. Suddenly the crew saw a man in a dazed and dishevelled condition come out of the 2nd class hatchway. It was Passepartout and this is how he had got aboard the ship: After falling unconscious in the tavern he had been lifted and put on a cot reserved for such people. Later on he started mumbling,

The crew saw a man in a dazed and dishevelled condition.

"Carnatic, Carnatic." Then the people guessed what he meant and put him aboard the ship. By now he became sober and remembered all that Fix had told him and how he had drugged him. Then he decided not to tell his master about it now but wait till they reached London.

Then he started looking for Mr. Fogg and Aouda and was told that they were not on board. This made him mad and he started crying and tearing his hair.

On the 13th the ship entered the harbour of Yokohama and Passepartout disembarked. He wandered all over the city wondering what to do till he reached the countryside and the paddy fields. By nightfall he had returned to the city feeling very hungry and came to the harbour.

PASSEPARTOUT, THE LONG NOSE

The next day Passepartout was very hungry and decided to find a job. So he thought that he should get some clothes more suited to a man who was hungry and looking for a small job. He entered a Japanese old clothes shop and explained the position to the manager. The manager liked his European clothes and gave him some money and an old faded Japanese robe and turban. He then had a good meal and went

Passepartout goes out to get some clothes.

to the harbour to find employment on a ship bound for America. As Passepartout neared the wharf he saw a poster announcing that Mr. William Batulcar's Circus Troupe was giving a last performance before leaving for United States. He looked for and found the office of Mr. Batulcar and after much argument and discussion he was hired as a clown and a Jack-of-all-work.

The acrobats performed all kinds of dangerous feats but the main attraction was the human pyramid in which our clown Passepartout was to take part. It was performed by the Long Noses. These performers had fixed long noses on their faces and instead of balancing on their shoulders as is usually done, balancing was to be done on their noses! They were all in position and the audience was applauding when suddenly the pyramid tottered and

He was hired as a clown.

crashed as one of the performers at the base, Passepartout, suddenly got up, jumped over the fence and fell at the feet of a spectator saying, “Ah, my master! my Master.” The spectator, as you may have guessed, was Fogg who, on seeing Passepartout, said, “What! you here !Well then, come to the ship with us.”

But the Honourable Batulcar was waiting outside and he asked for compensation for spoiling the show. Mr. Fogg threw him some notes and they left the circus with Passepartout still wearing his six-foot long nose!

The Long Noses.

THEY REACH SAN FRANCISCO

To go back a bit in this story, when the Yokohama bound ship which the Tankadere had signalled, saw the Tankadere it stopped alongside. Then Fogg explained the position to the captain, paid the money plus bonus to John Bunsby and also paid the captain of the ship to Yokohama and got on board en route for Nagasaki and Yokohama.

On disembarking he went straight to the

Carnatic and when he enquired about Passepartout he was told that he had arrived the previous day.

We know how Passepartout found Fogg and Aouda in the circus. The details about the voyage on the Tankadere were told to Passepartout by Aouda herself. When she mentioned that a man called Fix had accompanied them, he winced but did not tell them anything. The ship on which they were about to sail from Yokohama belonged to Pacific Mail Steamship Co. and was named General Grant. There were on board many Americans and Englishmen and several labourers emigrating to America.

Nine days after leaving Yokohama Fogg had crossed exactly one half of the Globe for, on the 23rd of November, the General Grant crossed the hundred and eightieth meridian. So Fogg had taken fiftytwo of the eighty

The ship crossed the hundred and eighteenth meridian.

days and had 28 days left to reach London. They had a very comfortable and safe sailing as the Pacific Ocean really lived up to its name and was very calm. They were happy that they were going back to more civilised countries and planned to catch the train from San Francisco to New York from where they would take a trans Atlantic liner to London which they would reach within the stipulated time.Fix was also on board but very depressed. On his arrival at Yokohama he had gone to the British Consulate and found that the warrant had arrived which had been despatched from Hong Kong but was forty days old and was now useless. Fogg had already left British soil and now could be arrested only on an extradition order so he decided to arrest Fogg in England. So he kept himself well away from Fogg and Aouda but one day Passepartout saw him on deck. He flew at him and gave him a good hiding which greatly amused the onlookers.When Passepartout had finished hammering Fix he was very relieved.

Fix said to Passepartout, "Now that you have given me a hiding, listen to what I say. So far I was your master's adversary, now I am on his side." "At last!" said Passepartout, "now do you believe him to be an honest man?"

"No, I still believe him a rogue. Till now I have been creating hurdles in his movements. I set the Bombay priests on him, I got you intoxicated at Hong Kong, I separated you from him and made him miss the boat," said Fix, "now I will help him to reach England as fast as possible.In England you will see whether your master is a criminal or an honest man. Now, are we going to be friends?"

He flew at him and gave him a good hiding.

“No’” replied Passepartout.

"No'" replied Passepartout, "allies, not friends. But at the slightest signs of treachery I will wring your neck!" "Agreed." said the detective. Eleven days later, on the 3rd December, the General Grant passed the Golden Gate and entered San Francisco. So far they had neither gained nor lost a single day.

CAUGHT IN THE ELECTION MELEE

At seven o'clock Fogg, Aouda and Passepartout landed on the floating pontoon quay of San Francisco. Passepartout was so happy that he landed with a somersault!

On landing Mr. Fogg enquired about the next train to New York and was told that it was at six that evening which gave them one full day to spend at San Francisco. They ordered a carriage to take them to a hotel.

Passepartout was anxiously looking out of the window to see the legendary city of 1849 with all its gold nuggets, assasins, gambling houses and sombreros. But all he saw was a modern town like any other. They passed low houses, churches, chapels, well decorated shops, warehouses and trams. They reached the hotel and saw that a table of dried meat,oyster soup, biscuits and cheese was laid for any one to eat free of charge.

They entered the restaurant and had breakfast after which Fogg and Aouda went to the English consulate to have their passports visaed. On the way they met Fix who told them that he would be travelling with them.

Suddenly there was heard a lot of shouting and two crowds came from opposite directions shouting slogans in favour of two

Crowds were shouting slogans.

candidates, one Mr. Kamerfield and the other, Mr. Mandiboy standing for election to a post of Justice of the Peace. When the two groups came to blows, Fogg and Aouda were caught in their midst and while trying to protect Aouda, Fogg bashed up a gentleman named Colonel Stamp Proctor and was challenged to a duel.

Somehow they got out of the melee, went to the hotel, had dinner, packed up and proceeded to the Station where the train was about to leave. They got in and took thier seats.

A BUFFALOE HERD STOPS THE TRAIN

The long train started from Oakland Station in San Francisco at six o'clock in the evening on their way to New York, a distance of three thousand seven hundred and eightysix miles and seven days to complete.

It goes through Omaha, Iowa, Kansas, Oregon and reaches Salt Lake City, the capital of the Mormon territory; from there it goes past Tuilla Valley, around the

American Desert, Mounts Cedar and Humboldt, the Sierra Nevada and the Andes to descend towards New York.

This what Phileas Fogg hoped to traverse in seven days to leave New York for Liverpool on the 11th. The train was made up of carriages without seperated compartments but with long rows of seats, a passage between them leading to the lavatories and dressing rooms. there were platforms out side each carriage on which one could walk the whole length of the train.There were saloon-cars, Balcony-cars, dining-cars and refreshment-cars and numerous vendors selling books and papers, drinks and eatables. At eight o'clock the Steward announced bed time and the carriage was converted into a dormitory with beds, clean sheets, blankets and pillows. As it was quite cold, the passengers were soon asleep.

They admired the scenery.

At seven in the morning, the train entered Cisco station and the carriage was again into its original state. After breakfast Fogg and his companions resumed their seats and were admiring the scenery when at about three in the noon a herd of about twelve thousand wild buffaloes started to cross the line making the train stop as it could not go through the herd.

The passengers were all watching this curious spectacle from the platforms but Passepartout was getting furious because of the delay. It took three hours for the herd to cross and then the train could start again. it eventually Utah at eight o'clock in the morning.

IN THE MORMON TERRITORY

During the night of the fifth of December the train neared the Great Salt Lake. Passepartout went on the platform for some fresh air at nine o'clock in the morning and was met by a man who introduced himself as Elder William Hitch, Mormon Missionary and who invited him to attend his lecture in carriage No.117 from eleven to twelve o'clock that morning. Passepartout entered the carriage at that time and took his seat.

Hitch came at eleven and exclaimed, "I tell you Joe Smith is a martyr. His brother Hiram is a martyr. The prosecutions of the Mormons by the U.S Government will make Brigham Young also a martyr!" Then he told the history of Mormonism which was a new religion started in Biblical times, how their Holy Book was written by Joseph Smith Junior who claimed to be a prophet in 1825 and said that the messenger from Heaven appeared to him and gave him the records of the Lord, how a temple was built at a cost of two hundred thousand dollars at Kirkland. In the end, Smith was ambushed by masked men, imprisoned and murdered. Most of the audience had left by now. By now the train had reached the Great Salt Lake or the Dead Sea, called so because it contains a lot of salt and no fish survive in it. The train arrived at Ogden at two o'clock and was due to leave at six so Fogg, Aouda and the other two went sight-seeing. The city was a typical American city with square, neat houses, surrounded by lovely gardens. The city was thinly populated with a majority of women as Mormon men are allowed to have more than one wife.

Just before four they returned to the train which left on time. As the train was picking up speed, a man came running fast and jumped on to the last carriage. when Passepartout asked him how many wives he had, he replied," only one and that too is more than enough. That's why I am running away!"

THE TRAIN DOES A LONG-JUMP

The train ran on till Weber River about nine hundred miles from San Francisco via the Rocky Mountains. It stopped at Fort Bridger Station and started immediately; it later entered Wyoming. That night there was heavy snowfall which worried Passepartout and he muttered, "What a mad idea to travel in winter. Could not my master wait till summer? It would give him a better chance." Aouda also was anxious but for a different reason. She had seen Colonel Proctor who had challenged Fogg, in the train.

When Fogg was sleeping she informed Fix who said,"Proctor on the train! Don't worry Madam, befor he settles with Mr. Fogg I will deal with him." "What is more, I will tackle him!" said Passepartout. So they decided that, somehow or the other they had to keep Fogg in the carriage occupied so that he would not meet Proctor. What better way than to organise games of Whist, Fogg's favourite game of cards? So Passepartout was sent to the steward to procure two packs of cards, scoring sheets, counters and a board covered with cloth. Aouda was a good player and was complimented by Fogg. Fix also was a very

Whist, Fogg's favourite game of cards.

good player and quite a match for Mr. Fogg. At eleven o'clock the train reached Bridger Pass, 7524 feet above sea level. The snow had stopped and the passengers had had their lunch. Suddenly the train stopped and they heard a long whistle.

The Watchman was saying to a group of passengers, "No, it is not possible to pass! The bridge at Medicine Bow is shaky as several chains are broken."

"Look here," said Colonel Procyor, "I suppose we are not going to be left here in the snow?" The guard said, "Colonel, we have telegraphed to Omaha for a train which will reach us in six hours." Passepartout was going sadly to inform his master when the engine driver, a typical Yankee said, "Gentlemen, there is one way by which we can get across, over the bridge

The jumping train.

by taking the train at full speed and making her jump over the bridge!" So all agreed to do so.

The guard shouted, "Take your seats." When all had done so, the driver got in and gave a long whistle while backing the train nearly one mile. There was a second whistle and the train started going faster and faster till it was practically flying at a hundred miles per hour.

The train flew over the bridge and shot five miles beyond the station before it could stop. But hardly had it crossed the river, when the bridge went down with a crash.

ATTACHED BY THE SIOUX

The train carried on, passing Fort Saunders, passed Evans Pass. They had now travelled 1302 miles in 3 days and 3 nights. During the night thay passed Walbach Camp. At 8 o'clock in the morning they passed Fort MacPherson.

Mr. Fogg and his partners were busy playing cards and Fogg was about to play a spade when a voice bellowed, "Hello Britisher!

You want to play a spade. I would play a diamond." Again he was challenged and Fix lost his temper and said he would fight the duel at which Fogg intervened and said it was his fight as Proctor had again insulted him. Then Fogg said," I am in a great hurry to reach England but I will come to America in six months and fight the duel. So give me a date." Proctor replied, "It shall be now and not after six months." Then it was decided that, as the train would stop for ten minutes at Plum Creek, they would fight there. As they reached Plum Creek the guard announced that the train was not stopping as they were already late and they may as well carry out their duel on the train itself. So now it was decided that they would fight in the aisle between the seats inside the carriage. Both the duellists and their seconds got ready when suddenly there were loud shouts and savage yells as, more than a hundred Sioux attacked the train.

The first thing the Sioux did was to kill the driver. The passengers also bravely fought back and killed many Sioux. The driverless train was gathering speed and the Guard, who was also wounded said that the train must be stopped before Fort Kearney station within five minutes. Passepartout at great risk to himself bravely went below the train and made his way to the engine and uncoupled it. As it started losing speed and the soldiers of Fort Kearney came running on hearing the firing, the Indians fled. When the passengers were counted on the platform it was found that several were missing, one of whom was the brave Passepartout.

The Sioux attack the train.

PASSEPARTOUT CAPTURED AND RESCUED

It was now seen that three passengers were missing. The wounded were many and Colonel Proctor was seriously wounded. Aouda and Fogg were alright and Fix was slightly scratched but Passepartout and two others were taken prisoner by the Sioux. Fogg said to the tearful Aouda," Whether alive or dead I will find him." So he approached the Captain of the garrison and told him to try and find the missing persons by following the Sioux. At first the Captain refused then Fogg said, "Very well then, I shall go alone."

The captain was so impressed that he agreed to go with thirty volunteers. Fogg told Fix to stay back and look after Aouda in case something happened to himself. As they started off, he told the soldiers, "My friends, there's a thousand pounds for you if we save the prisoners." At about two o'clock in the noon a whistle was heard and the engine was seen entering the station. It seems that the driver and stoker were only stunned and when they recovered, they stopped the runaway engine and brought it back and attached it to the train.the guard then announced that they would start immediately as they were already three

The captain was impressed.

hours late. So she and Fix decided to stay back. So the train left without them. They all passed a restless night waiting for the rescue party. In the morning the Captain was just deciding to send another detatchment after them when thay heard gunshots and saw Fogg leading the group which included Passepartout and the other two passengers. They were received with great joy by all. Phileas Fogg enquired about the train and was told that it had left the previous evening and the next one was due that same evening.

Fogg was leading the group.

THEY REACH THE HUDSON

Fogg was now 20 hours behind schedule. Passepartout was blaming himself for this delay and the loss of the wager. Just then Fix approached and said that he had found a way to continue the journey immediately. By sledge! So he took Fogg to a nearby hut and showed him a sledge with sails and rudder to steer.

They paid the owner for it and Fogg

They saw the sledge.

suggested to Aouda to stay back and follow by train as the journey would be hard but she insisited on accompanying them. So they all got in and Mudge, the owner unfurled the sail and the sledge flew on its way towards Omaha. After a gruelling journey and by one o'clock they had reached Omaha. They went straight to the station and got into an express train about to start.

The train went at a very high speed, passing through the State of Iowa, crossed the Mississippi and Illinois and Lake Michigan. They reached the Hudson at past eleven on the evening of the 11th December. They found that the China, bound for Liverpool had already sailed fortyfive minutes before!

NINE DAYS, THIRTEEN HOURS AND FORTY FIVE MINUTES MORE

Fogg's last hope seemed to have gone with the China. As there was no other ship due to leave for Liverpool immediately, they all went to a hotel in a dejected frame of mind as now, they were sure that the wager was lost. But Fogg was still calm. The next day Fogg went to the harbour. It was the 12th December. There were still nine days thirteen hours and fortyfive minutes for him to reach the Club. It looked as if he would fail. Then he happened to see a twin screw steamer anchored. He took a boat, went up to it on deck and asked for the Captain. A swarthy man approached him and said, "I am Andrew Speedy, the captain." "When do you sail?" "In an hour" said Speedy." "What is your cargo?" "Stones—no freight—going on ballast." "Will you take me and three passengers to Liverpool?" "No." said the Captain.

"I will charter her" "No." Fogg said then, "I will buy her."

"No."

Now Fogg offered him two thousand dollars each to which he readily agreed to take them upto Bordeaux. Then Fogg came ashore, rushed to the hotel, packed up and they boarded the ship Henrietta before 9 o'clock.

The Captain introduced himself.

FIX ARRESTS FOG

As soon as the ship sailed out of the harbour, Fogg started bribing the crew secretly till all were on his side and the real Captain was locked in his cabin and Fogg took over comand and gave orders to sail for Liverpool and not for Bordeaux. Fix was stunned by these developments. But thought that Fogg being a thief would not take the ship to Liverpool but to some other remote place. On the 13th they passed New

Foundland and the wind increased to a gale and they had to use extra fuel to keep the ship on course.

On the 16th the engineer came and told Fogg that they did not have enough fuel to reach Liverpool. On the 18th it was found that the fuel would be exhausted the same day. Fogg asked to bring the captain on deck. Captain Speedy came up fuming with rage and started shouting, "Pirate!, sea-robber!" Said Fogg to him, "Sir I called you to ask you to sell your ship to me." "No." shouted Speedy. "I shall have to burn her to get to Liverpool" said Fogg. Offering him sixty thousand dollars. He would burn only the wooden fittings, the cabins and so forth. The engine and all the iron work would be left for Speedy. The temptation of such an offer was too much for Speedy who readily agreed.

Fogg makes an offer to the Captain.

After using up the masts rafts and spars for fuel, on the 19th December they reached Queenstown. They waited for high tide for three hours and entered the harbour. Since Liverpool was still 24 hours away, Fogg decided to get off and catch the fast mail train Dublin and cross over to Liverpool in a fast boat. They shook hands with Speedy and disembarked, went to the station and took a fast train to Dublin from where they crossed over to Liverpool and landed at 20 minutes to twelve. He was now six hours from London. At this time Fix went up to him and said, "Are you Phileas Fogg?" "Yes I am." Fix said. "In the Queen's name I arrest you!"

FOGG FREED FROM PRISON

Fogg was confined in the Customs Lock-up. Passepartout and Aouda were distraught with sorrow when this happened and Passepartout would have assaulted Fix if the policemen had not held him. Now Fogg had lost the wager. Aouda and Passepartout stayed in the porch of the Custom House inspite of the cold. Fogg was sitting on the bench in the Cell placing his watch on the table . He thought of flight but when he examined the cell he found it was impossible. He wrote in his diary "80th day, 11.40 a.m" If he could get out now he could still make it to London in time. It was now two o'clock. At three minutes past two there was a great din outside and Passepartout, Aouda and Fix came rushing in towards him. Fix muttered, "Sir,-forgive me- most regrettable resemblance-thief arrested three days ago- you are free!"

Fogg stepped up to the detective, raised both his hands and gave him a good blow which felled him. "Well hit!" shouted Passepartout. The three of them then left Custom House, rushed to the station and found that the Express had left Liverpool for London already. It was fortyfive past two. Fogg engaged a special train which could leave at three only. Fogg attracted the driver with a reward and the train, going at high

Fogg hit the Detective.

speed,could have reached London in five and a half hours, but due to unforseen delays reached only at ten minutes to nine. Five minutes late! He had lost the wager by five minutes!

"I LOVE YOU AOUDA!"

From the station they went directly home and Fogg sent Passepartout to buy some provisions. Though he was ruined he was very calm. His complete savings of twenty thousand pounds were to be given to his fellow-members. Passepartout kept an eye on his master as he was afraid he would do something rash in his disappointment.

The next morning he did not go to the

"I love you Aouda."

Reform Club but sent for Aouda and said to her, “I had thought I would be a rich man so I brought you to England to settle you comfortably. But now I am ruined. Can you ever forgive me?” “Mr. Fogg, said Aouda, you saved me from death. I have no relatives or friends. You are all I have. Will you have me for a wife?”

Fogg was elated beyond words. He stood up and said, “I love you Aouda.” Mr. Fogg called Passepartout and asked him to call Reverend Samuel Wilson of Marylebone to solemnise the marriage the next day, Monday. “You want it tomorrow Monday?” “Yes, tomorrow, Monday.”

FOGG WINS £ 2000

The English public were full of admiration when it was announced that the real thief was not Fogg but James Strand, who was arrested by now. There were 3 days more for the 22nd December and since nothing had been heard of Fogg they wondered whether he was alive or dead. On Saturday the 21st December a huge crowd had gathered in front of the Reformer's Club and betting for and against Fogg was brisk.

It was now 8.40 and the Club members had already decided to deposit Fogg's cheque the next day.It was now 8.42, 8.43, 8.44. Now all were counting seconds!

At the 57th second, there was a great sound from the multitude and Phileas Fogg entered followed by a great crowd saying, "Here I am, Gentlemen!"

WEDDING BELLS RING

You will remember that Passepartout had been sent to inform Reverend Wilson to perform the marriage the next day, Monday. He was back in three minutes breathless and said, "Master, marriage impossible tomorrow—Sunday!" "But it is Sunday," said Fogg." "No," said Passepartout, "today is Saturday. We made a mistake of one day!" and he forthwith dragged his master by the collar, engaged a cab and thus they reached

Passepartout was breathless.

the Club at 8.45. Phileas had gone around the world in eighty days!

His mistake is easily explained. They had travelled ever Eastward. Going Eastward towards the sun gained him 4 minutes every one degree longitude.Thus through the earth's circumference of 360 degrees. 360 degrees multiplied by four make exactly twentyfour hours. That evening Aouda asked Fogg,"Now that you are rich, do you still want to marry me?" "Pardon me, my fortune is yours. If not for you Passepartout would not have gone to Rev. Wilson's house and we would have known the date and won the bet."

"Dear Mr. Fogg!"said Aouda. "Dear Aouda!" said Fogg. So Mr.Phileas Fogg had gone around the world in eighty days and won his wager. He had used every type of conveyance— liners, railways, carriages, yachts, trading vessels, sledges, elephants. He had gained a charming wife who had made him the happiest man on earth! And really, who would not go around the world for less?

Fogg marries Aouda.

EXCELSIOR!

A largely attended meeting, under the Presidentship of Sir Francis M....... was held at the Royal Geographical Society of London at 3, Waterloo Place on 14th January, 1862.

The audience consisted of veteran explorers who had undergone extreme hardship and dangers exploring the wilds of Polynesia and Africa and had been captured and tortured by the savages.

Sir Francis introduced one Dr. Ferguson who had a very bold scheme of exploring Africa for which the Society could vote funds; eventually a sum of two thousand five hundred pounds were voted. The audience then asked to see Dr. Ferguson, whereupon the Doctor was ushered in.

His eyes were gentle and intelligent, his arms were long and he did look like a great walker. He was applauded heartily by the gathering. He uttered one word,"Excelsior!"

Who was this Doctor? His father had been a captain in the British Navy and had associated his son with all the dangers he himself had faced and the boy developed a fearless and skillful way to deal with difficulties.

His imagination was fired by reading accounts of great explorers and men like Bruce, Selkirk and Robinson Crusoe. His father too, encouraged him by giving him a chance to study Hydrography, physics, mechanics, botany,medicine and astronomy.

After his father's death, young Ferguson had travelled a lot having joined many expeditions, with Captain Stuart in 1845, with Captain MacClure, exploring Tibet from 1855 to 1857 and his reputation as an intrepid explorer was enhanced. So there was no difficulty in the Society sanctioning him the money to venture on his latest and strange expedition.

After the meeting, dinner was served after numerous toasts were drunk to the success of the feat and in the honour of all the famous explorers of old.

The next day and the days to come the newspapers published many articles about the forthcoming expedition and many betted on its outcome.

DR. FERGUSON PLOTS THE ROUTE

Dr. Ferguson had a friend, Dick Kennedy who was so close to him that you could think they were two bodies but one heart. Dick was a Scot, living in the town of Leith; he was a fisherman and a marksman of the highest order. He was a six footer, graceful, with black eyes,a tanned complexion and very muscular. They had served together in the same Regiment in India. Dick was an expert hunter and Ferguson an expert botanist. Kennedy was wondering where Ferguson had disappeared when he read the report in The Daily Telegraph.

"Heavens Mercy!" he cried, "the fool! the madman! Cross Africa in a balloon! That evening Kennedy took the train from the General Railway Station and, on reaching London the next day, went straight to the Doctor's house in Soho. He knocked loudly and Ferguson himself opened the door.

"Dick? What are you doing in London in the shooting season?"

"I'm in London to stop a piece of great foolishness," said Dick, "is it true what this paper says? Are you really going to undertake this journey?"

"I do, my preparations are well ahead and I—"

Still Kennedy was refusing to accompany Ferguson on the expedition though Ferguson was insisting.

"If you want to cross Africa, why not do it the ordinary way?" asked Dick.

"Why?" answered the Doctor. "Because upto now all the famous explorers like Mungo Park, Vogel,Oudney, Major Liang and Roscher who tried it have been massacred by the savages. "

"Passing over would be alright, but flying over——"

"There's nothing to be frightened of," answered the Doctor,"I have taken all precautions to prevent the balloon falling down so don't worry. "

Now Kennedy was getting interested. He said, "Look here Samuel, have you found a way to steer the balloon?"

"No, but I will use the Trade Winds which blow from east to west. The British Government has placed transport at my disposal. Three or four ships also will cruise off the West Coast. Three months from now I will be at Zanzibar where I will inflate my balloon and we will launch her and——"

"We?" said Dick.

"Have you any objection now?" asked Ferguson.

"Objection! I've a thousand. So tell me: you say you can come down and go up as you please. In this way you will lose gas. Have you thought of this?"

"My dear Dick, I shall not lose an atom of gas, and I can come down or go up as I please. How this is done, is a secret. "

"All right. Excelsior!" answered the sportsman but in his mind he was determined to use all his power to deter his friend from undertaking this journey. As for Samuel, he went off to supervise preparations.

Ferguson then got busy in planning the route so as to link up the routes of Dr. Barth in 1849 and Speke and Burton's in 1858.

THE RELUCTANT KENNEDY

Dick was so scared of being up in the sky that some nights he used to have nightmares and fall off the cot! When he told the Doctor, the reply used to be, "Only three feet!" "Don't worry, we won't fall down." He used to shudder whenever Ferguson said, "WE are making good headway. . . . . . WE shall be ready on. . . . . . WE shall start on. . . . . " and, "OUR balloon. . . . . . OUR car. . . . . . OUR expedition. . . . OUR preparations. . .

. . . OUR" discoveries. . . . . OUR ascent. . . . . "

He still used to try to dissuade Ferguson asking if the discovery of the Nile was necessary or if the savages would be better off if they were to be civilised. This made the doctor angry who asked, "Do you want me to go back on my commitments? Do you want someone else to get all the glory? Is this the way you want me to show my gratitude to the Royal Geographical Society and the British Government for all they have done for me?"

Then Ferguson got a map and spread it in front of Dick and traced the route from Zanzibar on Lat. 6 degrees S . Now follow this parallel till Kazeh. Then follow the 33rd meridian till Lake Ukereue in lat. 2 degrees 30 min. S, 2 degrees above the Equator. From here, a stream runs and joins the Nile.

Now place the two points of a divider on these twoplaces. There are 2 degrees between them. This means a distance of only 150 miles! Nothing great! Do you know that, at this moment, the Geographical Society has sponsored an expedition lead by Captain Speke, along with Captain Grant and his soldiers to go up the lake till Gondokoro and John Petherick, the British at Khartoum has kept a ship ready with provisions at Gondokoro and wait for them. So we have no time to lose. And now, the Austrian Government has sent an expedition to look for Vogel who was sent to find Dr. Barth. Herr von Heuglin left in June to explore the Nile and link up Speke's and Barth's last points."

"Then why should we go?"asked Kennedy. Dr. Ferguson just shrugged his shoulders.

THE WEIGHING-IN

Dr. Ferguson had a servant, Joe, who was fully devoted to his master. He never grumbled or got angry. He loved and respected the doctor so much that he was ready to give his life for him. He was good at jumping, acrobats, climbing, flying and knew a bit of astronomy and botany having accompanied Ferguson on many expeditions. So, when he heard of the doctor's proposed journey, he was excited.

He said to Kennedy," Well, Mr. Kennedy,we are going to the moon. " Kennedy replied "I don't want to disappoint you, but he is not going. It is a mad scheme. Do you propose to accompany him?" "Yes, how can I let him go alone? Who will look after him if he falls ill? Who will help him? Moreover Africa is a wonderful place for a sportsman and hunter like you. You're coming with us."

"I'm coming with you at least upto Zanzibar to stop him from this foolishness."

Then the weighing of Kennedy—153 lbs, Joe—120 and Ferguson—135 lbs was completed.

THE CAR AND STORES MADE READY

Dr. Ferguson was busy with planning the expedition. As hydrogen is 14 1/2 times lighter than air and easy to produce, he decided to use hydrogen to inflate it. Then he calculated the weight to be carried to be 4000 lbs. and he had to work out lifting force to raise this weight.

A weight of 4000 lbs means an air displacement of 44,847 cubic feet, which means 44,847 cft of air weigh 4000 lbs. If the balloon had a capacity of 44,847 cft. and filling it with hydrogen, which would weigh only 276 lbs. The change of equilibrium would be 3780 lbs. This would be the lifting force.

But, if he filled it with 44,847 cft of hydrogen,it would expand fully on lifting and would be in danger of catching fire. So it is the usual practice to fill a balloon two thirds capacity. But Ferguson made a secret plan to fill it to only half it's capacity but since his load would be 4000 lbs. , he would make the balloon elongated in shape so now he would have a spheroid of 90,000 cubic feet.

Finally, he designed 2 balloons of unequal size, placing one inside the other connected by a pipe. This would increase chances of success as, if one balloon got damaged, the other would still fly.

The 2 balloons were made of twilled taffeta treated with gutta-percha, a kind of glue. Now the outer balloon weighed 650 lbs. and the inner balloon,510 lbs. totalling 1160 lbs. The net supporting the car was made of strong hemp rope and the car, circular in shape of diameter 15 feet and made of wicker-work strenghtened by iron casing and fitted with shock-absorbing springs, weighed 280 lbs together with the net.

Ferguson had two sheet-iron containers connected by pipes fitted with taps and a spiral tube 2 inches in diameter ending in 2 straight pieces, one 25 feet and the other 15 feet. there was also a powerful Bunsen battery. All this weighed 280 pounds. He had selected for the journey, 2 barometers,2 thermometers,2 compasses, 1 sextant,2 chronometers,1 theodolite and 1 alzimuth or binoculars. Also a ladder of strong silk 50 feet long and 3 iron anchors. Also 2 drinking-water iron containers, each of 22 gallon capacity and a good supply of brandy.

His stores would be tea,salt meat, coffee, biscuits and pemmican. He had an awning over the car and blankets and sporting guns,powder and shot.

His calculations of weight are as follow (in pounds)

Ferguson	135
Kennedy	153
Joe	120
Outer balloon	650
Inner balloon	510
Car and net	280

Anchors, instruments, guns and blankets	190
Coffee, brandy and water	400
Apparatus	700
Weight of hydrogen	276
Ballast	200
Tent and other gear, meat, tea, pemmican and biscuits	386
TOTAL	4000 pounds

The ballast was to be used only in emergency.

By February end they were ready.

FAREWELL FUNCTIONS

The hull of the ship had been modified so as to carry the balloon. The car,anchor, ropes, stores and other containers as well as 10 barrels of sulphuric acid and 10 of scrap iron to produce hydrogen were also taken aboard.

Two cabins were kept ready for Kennedy and Ferguson. Ferguson took with him, 2 DBBL guns, 1 carbine, 2 Colt revolvers and plenty of shot and powder. On 18th February, the three went aboard. Joe was put in the crew quarters. On 20th, a grand dinner was arranged for Dr. Ferguson and Kennedy by the members of the Royal Geographical Society. The ship's officers also were invited. A lot of speeches were made and toasts were drunk. During the party, a message was received from the Queen with good wishes for their successful expedition.

At 5 a.m. 21st Feb., the Resolute sailed with the three on board, lock, stock and barrel.

The next morning, 21st February at 5 a. m,the Resolute sailed. Ferguson later explained the history of previous expeditions to Africa by Barth, Speke, Grant, Burton and others.

THE MODE OF RISING AND DESCENDING

On the 30th March, the Resolute reached Cape Town, but stopped only to take coal.

The captain asked Ferguson one day, "How will you steer your balloon?" "No method has yet been found, so we have to depend on air currents to carry us. So we have to go up and down and find the currents,"the doctor replied. "But how will you go up and down?" "To ascend we will throw out some ballast and to come down we will let out some gas." "But this method has not yet been discovered," the captain said.

"It has," replied Ferguson, "by me. I did not announce this in England as it would have started a public argument." "Then what is your secret?"

"It is this, gentlemen, and very simple." Ferguson went on to explain.

“IT MAY BE DANGEROUS

Many have tried to develope a way to rise and descend at will but none has succeeded.

So I devised my own way by expanding or contracting the gas whwnever I want.

I have 5 containers. The first containing 25 gallons of water,with a few drops of sulphuric acid. This, I decompose by means of the Bunsen battery. Water as you know breaks up into oxygen and hydrogen due to electrolysis. Oxygen is collected in a separate container from the positive pole of the battery and hydrogen, from it's negative pole, in a third container, bigger than the other. These two containers are connected to a fourth container by taps. This is the mixing container of 41 cubic feet. The upper part is fitted with a platinum tube fitted with a tap.

This is the first part of my apparatus. The second part is : From the lower part of the balloon 2 tubes come out. One from the upper part of the balloon and the other from the lower. They reach the car and enter a chamber called the heating chamber closed at both ends by 2 strong discs. The pipe from the lower part of the balloon enters the chamber through the lower disc. This is the same as central heating of a home. When the heating apparatus is lit, the gas enters the upper part of the balloon to keep it up.

So you see,when I want to rise, I heat the gas to a temperature higher than that surrounding it and when I want to descend,I just lower the heat of the furnace. I am also taking some ballast with me for emergencies.

This is my secret, gentlemen,only expansion and contraction of the gas." With this, Ferguson finished. The captain said, "But it may be dangerous."

"So what," said Ferguson, "as long as it is practicable".

KENNEDY MAKES A DECISION

They reached Zanzibar at 11 a.m. on 15th April and arrangements were made for them to stay as guests of Imam of Muscat.

Their baggage was taken to the consul's house but when it came to unloading the balloon, the consul told them that the local poulation,being fanatics who worship the sun and moon may think that a European was going up in the air to harm these heavenly bodies. The doctor said, "Then what shall we do? All our efforts would come to naught if they damage the balloon."

The consul then told them that there was an island nearby where they could unload the balloon and assemble it. His soldiers would guard the place. This plan was accepted and thay sailed to the nearby island. Two 80-foot masts were put up 80 feet apart and by means of a pulley system the inner balloon was fixed to the outer balloon and both were lifted at the same time.

On the 17th, they loaded stones like dilute sulphuric acid, iron ropes, anchors, tents, instruments, guns, water and ballast.

Seeing these preparations, the natives were getting more and more furious and shouting and dancing. They were being incited by their witch doctor.

At six that evening the travellers attended a farewell dinner on board ship and slept on the ship itself. At 6 a. m they went to the island. Captain Pennet and the officers bade farewell and good luck to them.

Kennedy went up to the doctor and said, "So, Samuel, is it settled that I am coming?" "Yes, old man." said the doctor. "I've done all in my power to stop this expedition?" Kennedy asked "Everything." Fergus on replied. "Then I can come with an easy conscience!" said Kennedy.

At 9 a. m the three climbed in the car. The doctor lit the flame and the gas started to heat up. Slowly the balloon started to rise. When it rose to 20 feet Kennedy shouted, "My friends, I christen this airship Victoria!"

The Victoria climbed to 1500 feet and entered a current taking it in a southwesterly direction. From the sky they enjoyed the beautiful scenery of Zanzibar below. The gas got further heated by the sun's rays and the Victoria climbed to 2500 feet.

They passed our barley, maize, rice and tobacco fields at 300 feet. They ccould see the villagers shouting.

GOING ON A HUNT

Kennedy woke up in the morning with a slight temperature. So Joe freed the anchor and they rose. Already the temperature had dropped and the ground could not be seen. Soon Kennedy's fever left him and he ate well, they were going at 20 miles per hour and at about 10 a.m. the mist cleared and the earth was visible. The Victoria dropped some more and they found a current six hundred feet above ground level in a northward direction and soon they were among the mountains which worried Kennedy but the doctor said, “Don’t worry, Dick, we will not run aground. “The doctor was steering the balloon expertly. He said, “If we were journeying by land, we would have to struggle over marshes, through water, our animals would have perished, we would be constantly quarelling with our porters, and attacked by flies, mosquitos, wild animals and savages. It is not exaggeration but travellers have told stories which you would shiver if you heard.”

By eleven o’clock they were over the Rubehos, “We will have to go up over 5000 feet and clear them. ” said the doctor.

So the gas was heated and the balloon rose easily and the barometer read a height of 6000 feet.

Ferguson explained,"Earth's atmosphere extends to a height of 6000 fathoms. Brioschi and Gay-Lussac did go above this height but started bleeding from ears and mouth. Two Frenchmen also tried it but their balloon tore and they fell to the ground. But don't worry, we will not fall but I have got some sense and will stop at a safe height."

At this height the air was thin and sound carried badly and the eyesight became poor. Soon the Victoria skirted the ridge and they dropped anchor to a big tree.

"Now," said Ferguson, "you and Joe take two guns and shoot some antelope."

THE NATIVES ATTACK

The country was a wilderness with caravan tracks with bones of men and animals here and there. Dick and Joe were were stumbling along when Dick sighted some antelopes grazing. Dick stalked them and took aim and fired. One splendid blaubok fell dead. It was bluish-grey with white belly and legs.

Kennedy said," This is a very rare

specimen, I will keep the skin." "But the doctor will never allow extra weight, sir." said Joe, "so I will cook it here which will please Dr. Ferguson." And he cut some tender meat from the animal and grilled them over the fire. Suddenly they heard a shot and picked up their bags and ran towards the balloon when they heard another shot.

"Hurry up." said Joe, "there's another shot"

"Looks like he is defending himself. Come on!" and they ran faster when Joe said,"Good Lord! The master will be finished, look there, niggers are attacking him. "

After a mile, they heard one more shot from the car and one ruffian dropped lifeless. Then they saw that it was only a band of monkeys! But Dick said, "Hurry up."

They reached the car, freed the anchor, got in and rose up to safety and enjoyed the antelope flesh.

It was 4 o'clock and the Victoria began to lose height due to a current so the doctor increased the heat of the burner so she rose. At 7 o'clock they were over the Kanyemi basin which is ruled by a Sultan.

After Kanyemi the area became rocky, then again greenery appeared near Mdaburu. At night, since they could not find a suitable tree to anchor, they slept in the car itself. The night was cold. Jackals and tigers could be heard. The Victoria was now over Mabunguru with its beautiful rocks. Bleached bones of elephants and buffaloes could be seen here and there. Trees were few.

At 7 o'clock they saw a round rock. "There's Jihoue la Mkos, let's anchor and get some water." The doctor suggested. Since there were no suitable trees, they anchored to a rock. According to the map, there were great lakes here so Joe set off with a cask which he filled and returned. He brought back a strange fruit which the doctor said was of the 'mhenbu' tree. When Joe returned, the doctor increased the flame and the Victoria rose again. As the level of the land was about 3000 feet, it became difficult to control the balloon without expanding the gas too much so the doctor skillfully steered above a slope and over the villages of Thembo and Tura Wels and at 2 o'clock they were above the town of Kazeh.

The doctor announced, "We left Zanzibar two days ago at 9 a. m and have travelled nearly 500 miles which took Burton and Speke four and a half months." We will now descend into the market of Kazeh."

THE LADIES WORSHIP JOE

When the villagers saw the Victoria in the sky gently descending and they all ran and hid in fright. Kennedy said that if they frightened folks that way they would not be able to do any business.

"Don't worry, the natives will get over their fright and slowly return. "

Are you then thinking of talking with them Samuel?" said Kennedy.

"Surely," replied Ferguson, "there will be some educated Arabs in Kazeh. Burton and Speke spoke highly of these people." As they anchored to a tree in the market place, the whole crowd including witch-doctors, men women and children came out and stretched their arms skywards in a pious manner.

"That's their way of worshipping; Joe, you will be playing the role of a god now." said the doctor. "That is fine, sir, I like the smell of incense!"

Then the 'myanga' or witch-doctor and all were silent. He addressed the travellers in an unknown language and the doctor replied in Arabic which was understood by him. The man gave a speech to the crowd saying that the Victoria was the Moon and these were her three sons come down to bless their village.

The doctor replied that once every 1000 years they visited Earth to fulfil the desires of the people so they could express their desires. They then asked the doctor to cure their chief who was very ill to which Ferguson agreed and told them to inform the chief to get ready to receive them.

"Now Dick will stay in the balloon and Joe at the foot of the ladder but be prepared to make a run for it if need be. I am going with some medicines. They are superstitious so I will be safe; but don't desert your posts. Watch the gas expansion." The crowd was shouting louder now.

Ferguson took his medicine chest and, accompanied by loud music and a large crowd, was met by the son of the Sultan who prostrated himself before the Son of the Moon, and proceeded to the palace where he was respectfully received by all.

They entered the palace where he was received by all the Sultan's wives to the beating of upatu, a type of copper cymbal and klindo, a type of drum out of a tree trunk. The women were pretty and wore long robes with a kilt in front and always smiling. But six of them were sitting sadly. They were to be buried alive with the Sultan to keep away his loneliness! Ferguson noticed all this. On the bed, he saw that the Sultan, about 40 years old,was a victim of drink and debauchery and nothing could save him. He administered a dose of strong medicine which made the Sultan stir a bit which made the crowd shout in the doctor's honour. This gave a chance to the doctor to slip out of the palace.

Meanwhile the ladies were worshipping Joe and offering gifts and fruit and beer to him. He was enjoying the attention. The girls began dancing round him. Not to be outdone, he too started dancing a jig which the natives imitated thinking it to be the dance of the gods in the Moon. Just then Ferguson came rushing and started to climb up the ladder followed by Joe who was worried. "We have to get away immediately, cut the anchor loose." said the doctor, "the moon has come out and the natives might suspect us to be imposters." Then the anchor was cut and they rose.

THE BALLOON CAUGHT IN A STORM

"At 8 o'clock they were in Long. 32 degrees 40 minutes E, Lat. 4 degrees 17 minutes S and above Mfuto. "This is called the Moon Country." said the doctor. Joe asked, "Why are such beautiful places in wild countries?"

"How do know that one day civilisation may not reach here? You read in history that all the most fertile lands exhaust their fertility after many days and people move on to wild places and make them yeild rich harvests in time. Europe, America and parts of Africa are examples. The whole of the wilds of Africa will also follow one day and become very populous and fertile and will become a great kingdom. "Kennedy said.

"How nice! I wish I could live to see it. " said Joe.

Moreover, industries and machines are getting a hold on everything till one day man will invent one great boiler which will blow up and destroy the world!" said Kennedy. Joe added, "I bet the Yankees will invent that fatal boiler. "

"Possible. But let us discontinue this argument and enjoy the scenery of the Country of the Moon." said Ferguson.

They could see huge trees and small

hillocks. The Mlagarasi, a tributary of Lake Tanganyika could be seen winding it's way among the jungles and hills. Lions, leopards, hyenas and tigers lurked in the tall grass. Even elephants could be heard.

"What a country for hunting! You could just lift your gun and fire and you would surely hit an animal. "said Kennedy, "can we try?"

"No," replied Ferguson, "it is late and also there'll be a terrible storm now." "Would it not be a good idea to get down?"asked Kennedy.

"I would rather go up, because, during these storms,the earth is charged with electricity. I shall steer towards the latitude of the Nile source. We are now in Long. 32 degrees 40 minutes and I want to fly straight across the Equator." said the Doctor, "and pick up some signs of Speke's expedition."

"You better sleep, sir, we will keep watch." said Joe.

"Thank you Joe. Goodnight, I hope. We are stationary, I may wake you in this same place in the morning." Soon after Kennedy and Joe went to sleep it became very dark and lightning flashed and the rumble of thunder shook the sky.

Ferguson woke them both up saying, "If we go down the balloon will be destroyed so we have to rise before the wind rises and the clouds burst." Just as he said this, rain started and the sky was full of electric flashes.

"It's too late. Now we will have to pass through fire with a combustable gas in our balloon." "Take her down! Down to earth!"

shouted Kennedy. "That is also too risky," replied Ferguson. "We're rising, sir. "said Joe. "God help us." We're in His hands. Pray hard for help from Him." said Ferguson.

The balloon was being tossed around like a kite and rising amid the lightning and hail. The barometer showed a height of 1000 feet. It was 11 p. m.

As the Victoria kept rising, 15 minutes later they were safe above the storm and approached the mountains towards Lake Tanganyika.

A MEAL OF ELEPHANT MEAT

Kennedy asked, "Are we going to cross them?" "No, I hope to find a good wind and cross the Equator. If necessary I will anchor the balloon till we do." Soon, a north-West current rose and they ran at a good speed as they wanted. "Are we going like this for long or can we land and stretch our legs?" asked Kennedy. "Yes," replied Ferguson, "we will have to be careful with our stores and you,

Dick will supply us with fresh meat. Also, we have to get fresh water as we may cross waterless areas." By lunch they were in long. 29 deg. 15 min. E, lat. 3deg. 15 min. W near the Equator. The tribes here were friendly so they decided to land and overhaul the balloon. There were no trees so they trailed the anchor till it caught in a fissure in the rock. Suddenly the rock started to move and they saw it was an elephant! It started running to shake off the anchor caught between it's tusks. But luckily it was running in the direction they were travelling. Now they saw a forest a bit ahead and the elephant was going straight there. Kennedy fired at it to kill it but it ran faster. At last one bullet pierced it's eye and it stopped. Then he fired again and it fell dead.

One tusk snapped. Kennedy wanted to

take the tusk as it would fetch a lot of money but Ferguson said, "No, old man, we're not ivory traders and have not come here to make money and become rich!" Joe and Ferguson jumped down and approached the dead tusker. Joe said, "What a splendid animal!" "Yes," said Kennedy, "Central Africa has the finest elephants. Those of India are much smaller."

"Mr. Kennedy can go hunting while I prepare a delicious meal of elephant meat while Dr. Ferguson inspects Victoria. "said Joe. All agreed to Joe's proposal.

Joe then dug a hole, filled it with dry branches, lit a fire and when the hole was very hot,he put the tenderest parts of the mastodon and covered it with another fire. When it was cooked, he arranged a feast on the grass,with coffee, brandy and some biscuits. Dr. Ferguson, meanwhile, inspected the balloon and found that it had luckily escaped damage. Just then, Kennedy returned with some partridges and the leg of an oryx or type of antelope. They enjoyed the meal and drink, smoked some Havanas then built fires round them to keep away wild animals and enjoyed a sound sleep. At 5 a.m. they got up and cast anchor and rose up and below them the land was dry with very few fields of rice, barley and plantain. This was the land of Karagwah. They could see the inhabitants looking upwards at them in surprise. At noon Victoria was above Lake Victoria Nyanza and began to cross the lake northwards. There were millions of mosquitoes along the banks and herds of hippopotamus could be seen in the reeds. The winds were quite strong here and they held course with difficulty. They could not land due to the mosquitoes so they just moored to a tree. They let as munch rope as possible as the mosquitoes had begun to rise. At 4 a.m. they were above the Equator.

So they celebrated with a toast. The wind was now blowing strong and they could see a few craft on the lake while crossing it." I'm sure this is the source of the Nile. "said Ferguson. "We will see soon." said Kennedy. At nine o'clock the west bank closed in and they could see the other bank. Dr. Ferguson closely examined the country.

"Look, friends, The stories of the Arabs were true. They said a river by which Lake Ukereue poured it's water northwards. We are now following the river. It is the Nile!" he said. "It's the Nile!" shouted Kennedy and Joe cried, "Hurrah!"

"But how will we be sure of the identity

of the river with that seen by the travellers from the north?" asked Kennedy. "We shall soon have proofs if the wind remains favourable for another hour." said Ferguson. The mountains passed and they came over villages where the tribes were hostile and regarded the foreigners not as gods and felt that they had come to rob them of something by discovering the Nile; so the Victoria kept out of the range of their muskets.

"I have to go down somewhere here to confirm the results of our expedition. At least for 15 minutes." said the doctor. Kennedy said, "If it comes to shooting we, your guards, are ready."

"We will first rise a bit to study the land." said Ferguson. The hydrogen was heated and the balloon rose to 2500 feet and after a while Victoria was brought down to less than 100 feet and following the course of the Nile; the doctor was examining the ground searching for a landmark he knew about. They could also see the natives following them but Kennedy scared them away with a shot. Suddenly Ferguson was looking through the glass at an island below them.

"Four trees!" he cried, "look there. It must be Denga." Four trees could be seen. He added, "That's where we have to go down." "But it's inhabited." said Kennedy; the natives could be seen gathered with arms. "We'll make them run," said Ferguson. "Whereupon Kennedy fired a few shots and the natives fled. The ladder was let down, "Follow me Kennedy, I want a witness, Joe, keep a look- out." Saying which, the doctor and Kennedy jumped down and went to a cluster of rocks. The doctor searched among rocks and thorns. Suddenly he cried, "Look!"

Kennedy looked down at the rock's face and saw two letters etched clearly:

" A.D. "

"A.D, Andrea Debono. The traveller who got nearest to the source of the Nile."

"It is the Nile. Now there's no doubt about it. Back to the balloon."

They returned to the balloon and rose up and continued on their journey after Ferguson hoisted the Union Jack!

HOW MADAME BLANCHARD DIED

"I can see some waterfalls." said Kennedy. Ferguson replied, "They are the Falls of Makedo and that mountain you see there is Longwek. The tribes there are enemies and are always fighting. These were the dangers that Debono faced. Now we are crossing Africa in real earnest. Till now we have been following our predecessors. Now we will enter the unknown. Are you ready to face it?"

"Yes!" cried Kennedy and Joe as one. "Then off we go. May God help us on our journey!"

At 10 p. m they crossed the Trembling Mountains. Now they had 315 miles on this the 23rd April. Kennedy and Ferguson were very silent and deep in thought. May be they were thinking about these discoveries. At 11 p.m the Victoria moored. the travellers had a good meal and slept by turns while one kept watch. Next day they got up early,had breakfast and continued in very good weather and a helpful wind.

"We are now crossing Usega," said the doctor, "geographers had heard from the Arabs that there used to be a lake here. We have made many sketch maps of the area. Now we will see and correct if needed." "Is this place inhabited?" asked Joe. "Yes, with cannibals. It was said that they had tails but that was because of the animal skins they wore. They are ferocious and love human meat. They are called Nyam Nyams, the sound of eating!" "I hope they won't be keen to eat me. If I've got to be eaten in case of necessity, I would rather be eaten by my master or you, Mr. Kennedy and not by some savages."

By now a thick mist arose and they could not see the earth. The night was calm but in the morning strong winds blew and tossed the balloon about. They tied the ropes securely so that it would not catch fire due to escaping hydrogen.

"Will we be dashed to the ground?" asked Kennedy.

"No," said Ferguson, "if the gas escaped we will come down slowly. Such an accident took place with Madame Blanchard. As she let off fireworks, the hydrogen caught fire and her balloon floated down gently but hit a chimney and she fell to her death." "Hope that will not happen to us." said Kennedy.

"Yes," said the doctor, "accidents are caused only by our carelessness; it is most dangerous during lifting and landing. So we have to take all safety measures."

THE CANNIBALS

Just then the Victoria was approaching a forest of huge and tall banyan trees more than 300 feet tall so they had to ascend above the trees. After the forest came a cluster of huts arranged in a circle. There was a single tree in the centre at the base of which were heaped a lot of human bones.

"That is a war tree of the cannibals," explained the doctor, "The flowers you see in the branches are the freshly cut heads of enemies!"Later on they saw numerous half eaten human corpses with hyenas and jackals feeding upon them which, the doctor said, were the bodies of criminals who were killed and torn apart by animals. "If this is cruelty, we can also call hanging cruelty. Some tribes shut criminals with their animals in their hut and set fire to them; that is also cruelty, is it not?" said Ferguson.

As night approached, they mooned to a tree and retired. At midnight Kennedy heard a hissing sound and woke the other two. "Some more monkeys?" asked Joe. "Possibly," Kennedy replied, so Joe and I will go down and keep guard." "And I will make preparations to get away fast if necessary." said the doctor. Dick and Joe then slowly climbed down and waited in silence. They again heard a rustle and Joe said, “It may be a snake.” “No it is humans.”

A few savages were actually climbing up the tree stealthily. As two heads came up, Kennedy fired and the savages fled howling. But then they heard a voice crying,”Help! Help!” in French. The doctor said, “A frenchman in the hands of these savages! We must help him. He may have heard our shot and thought help was at hand.

We cannot disappoint him. As soon as it is light we will do something.” Again the voice crying, “Help! Help!.” was heard.

“Suppose they kill him in the night?”Joe asked but Ferguson said that the savages usually killed in the light. but still Joe and Dick were unconvinced.

They said they could creep up silently and save the prisoner to which the doc objected. "Dick, I beg of you do what I say. Supposing they capture you also? We will have to rescue two instead of one." But they were begging to do something to save the poor prisoner. The doctor then took up the megaphone and shouted in French, "You there! Take heart, you have three friends looking after you." A loud roar answered him, drowning his reply. "If there was light," said the Scot.

"I would go down and fire my gun and chase them away." "And you Joe?"

"I would write a note to the prisoner to run in a certain direction,tie it to an arrow and fire it to him."

"Your plans would not succeed. But yours,Dick,may succeed taking advantage of their fear of the noise of guns. But if it failed and they captured you? So we will try another plan. All the chances must be on our side. There are 200 lbs. of ballast left. Suppose this man weighs as much as one of us,we will have 60 pounds for a fast rise. "What do you mean?" asked Kennedy.

"This,"replied Ferguson, "if I throw out ballast equal to the prisoner's weight,the balloon's balance will be stable but if we want to rise fast we will have to use something more drastic that the burner. The disadvantage is that if I want to come down later I will have to lose the same amount of gas which is precious. But we must sacrifice something to save a precious life. So hurry, place those sacks round the edge of the car to push them out fast."

"What about the darkness?" asked Kennedy.

"It will hide our preparations. Get all the

guns ready so we will have 17 shots fired at the same time from one carbine, two revolvers and two guns." said Doc. Joe was told to be ready to throw the ballast and Dick to get the prisoner.

Then the doctor took two ends of the conducting wire and fixed a sharpened piece of carbon to each and brought the points together. Suddenly a vast sheet of light destroyed the blackness of the night. "Oh! Sir!" said Joe. "Shh" Doc said.

Looking down, they saw a priest bleeding and tied to a stake and decided to rescue him.

THE PRIEST IS RESCUED

As soon as this was done, the car slowly started going down. The light had scared everyone into hiding so the square was empty. Kennedy jumped down, picked the man and jumped back into the car.

Some of the bolder negroes, seeing this, approached the car. After a few feet the car suddenly stopped. they were wondering why when Joe cried out, "One of the brutes is hanging on to the rope." Dick took up the water container and threw it at the fellow who fell off.

The balloon immediately climbed to 1000 feet. "Hurrah!" shouted Joe. The doctor then separated the two points and it again became dark. It was 1 a. m. the prisoner opened his eyes.

"You are safe, don't worry." Ferguson told him.

"Saved from a cruel death," he replied. But my end has come,I have not long to live." And he again fell back in a faint.

"He's dying!" cried Dick. "No," Ferguson replied. But he is very weak. let him rest. put him under the tent. "They then laid him in the tent and Ferguson prepared some medicine and poured a few drops on his lips. Then they gave him a sponge bath after cleaning his many wounds and blood and let him sleep.

At daylight the Victoria drifted with a current west-north-west. Kennedy went and looked at the priest and said,: I hope we can save this poor man. Is there a chance?" "Yes," said Ferguson, "with care. The air is so pure."

They watched him throughout the day and night when the Victoria was moored. The next morning he recovered a little to speak. Ferguson asked, "How do you feel?"

"A bit better. I do not know what happened. Who are you so that I can remember you in my last prayer." "We are English travellers," Ferguson replied, "crossing Africa in a balloon. While passing,we were lucky enough to save you." "Science has it's heroes," said the priest. "Religion has it's martyrs." added Dick.

"I'm a priest of the Lazarist Mission. God be praised for sending you to me. For 5 years I have been among the savages. I have had no news of the outside world all these years. Tell me about Europe and France." the priest requested.

Ferguson told him all about Europe and France also feeding him lots of tea.

"You are very brave men." he said, "you will succeed in your enterprise." Then he told them about himself in French. He was from a village in Brittany. When twenty years old, he became a priest and came to Africa to work among the savages. Though they rejected his teachings and treated him cruelly, he continued teaching. When the chief died,they blamed him and sentenced him to death. When they were about to kill him, he was rescued by the travellers.

A DEATH IN THEIR CAR

"Raise me to my knees, I beg you." They raised him to his knees.

"God have mercy on me," cried the dying priest and he fell dead.

Ferguson said sadly, "Tomorrow we will bury him here where his blood was shed." The next day they wre passing over a land full of craters and ravines.

At noon, to have the burial,Ferguson

lowered the balloon in a ravine. But as they had lost ballast while rescuing the priest, Joe got down and placed a lot of large rocks in the balloon as ballast.

"What are you thinking of, Sam?" asked Kennedy.

"The strange contrast in Nature. The priest who had taken the vow of poverty is now resting in a gold mine." "A gold mine!" Exclaimed the two others. You will find gold in these fissures if you remove the stones." Ferguson told them. Immediately both of them threw themselves on the rocks and gathered a big pile of them to take away. The doctor said, "Steady Joe, what is the use of all this gold to us? We can't take it away. It is too heavy for our car. I should not have told you about the gold."

"Can we at least take the gold as ballast?"

asked Joe, to which the doctor said "All right, I agree. But you may have to throw out some of it." So Joe started loading about a thousand pounds of ore into the car and cast a last look on the grave of the priest. There was no wood to erect a cross.

Ferguson was more worried about water because they had lost a lot of water when they threw the barrel on the savage trying to climb up the rope.

They got into the car and the doctor lit the burner. Though the hydrogen heated, the balloon would not rise. Joe was watching uneasily but was silent.

"Joe." called the doctor. No reply. "Joe, can you hear me? be good enough to throw out some of these rocks."

"But, sir, you said I could———" "I said to replace the ballast only. The balloon will not rise with all this weight. Do you want us to stay in this desert forever?" Ferguson asked. Joe very reluctantly threw some overboard but still the balloon would not rise." Throw some more!" said the doctor," At least 400 lbs. which Joe did and the balloon started rising.

THEY SEE ANOTHER BALLOON

As their water was low because of the barrel which was thrown at the savage, they were worried and silent. Joe was worried about the gold in the car which, though valueless now, would be priceless tomorrow.

They had entered the desert now. There was no vegetation and they could see only stones, sand and a few shrubs. There were also no animal or human bones to be seen.

But the worst thing was there were only three gallons of water with them. Ferguson kept one gallon for drinking and two gallons to feed the burner. That means, they had water for only 54 hours of travel. he also rationed the drinking water. They also stopped at night and travelled during daytime so as not to miss spotting water sources.

The night was hot but peaceful and the day was extremely hot. They could have avoided the heat if they rose higher but this would mean using more water which was precious. So the doctor kept at a height of 100 feet above ground.

The doctor was very depressed. He looked all the time for water through the glass. He was feeling the responsibility too much. He had brought these two good friends to face such hardship and may be, destruction. Could they turn back? Or could they face the possible hardships ahead?He asked them if they wished to go back. Joe replied, "I will go whereever my master goes. I will suffer whatever he suffers."

"What about you Kennedy?" asked Ferguson to which Kennedy replied, "I am with you body and soul, Samuel. I feel that we should go till the end. Anyway, it is too late to return so we will go forward." "Thank you, friends, I am grateful." said Ferguson and the three friends shook hands. "According to my calculations we are 300 miles from the Gulf of Guinea. If we proceed towards the coast we may find some oasis with water. We could do with a stiff wind."

The next day they saw a cloud but still no rain. Then a strange thing happened, another balloon with three passengers' was seen which turned out to be only a mirage. They then descended spent the night down.

JOE OFFERS TO SACRIFICE HIMSELF

The Victoria covered only 10 miles the previous day. The next morning the doctor got ready for departure and announced, "We have only 6 hours for the burner to hold out. If we don't find water before that, the burner will give out. "Joe said,"Perhaps there will be a wind soon."

It was wishful thinking! There was absolutely no wind. The temperature was 113 degrees. They were in agony due to thirst and could not quench their thirst on brandy alone as they had only two pints of drinking water left! Ferguson was repenting of having wasted 2 gallons of water by decomposing. That much water would have given them 9 more days of travel. But gas was the blood of the balloon.

These thoughts were revolving in his head. Then he decided to make one last and final attempt to find a breeze to take them forward. While Joe and Kennedy were sleeping, he raised the temperature of the gas high and the balloon rose to a height of 1000 feet but there was no wind. At last the water finished and the burner died down bringing the balloon gently to earth. Their position was now 6 degrees 51 minutes N and 19 degrees 35 min. E 500 miles from Lake Tchad and 400 miles from the African coast.

When night fell the doctor suggested taking a short walk but the other were too weak to do so, so the doctor went alone. After a few miles, he suddenly felt giddy and he fell unconscious on the sand.

At midnight he regained consciousness to find himself in the arms of Joe who had found him by following his tracks. Joe helped him return to the Victoria.

"You should not try these things, sir," said Joe, "We can't go on like this. One of us should sacrifice himself for the rest and that one should be me."

"What do you propose?" Ferguson asked.

"It is simple. I will take some food and start walking straight ahead until I reach some Arab village., Meanwhile, if you get a favourable wind, go without me, and if I find a village I will bring help to you or I will die."

"It's a mad idea but does you credit, Joe. But we will not allow it," replied Ferguson. Joe said that he would wait one more day.

SEARCHING IN VAIN FOR WATER

In the morning the doctor first consulted the barometer but found no change in it. The searing heat and absence of wind was still prevailing.

Kennedy got up very ill. His tongue was blistered and he could hardly talk. He was walking up and down crying hoarsely, then he went into a coma.

By evening Joe also started halucinating.

He imaged the sand to be a pool of water and fell down to drink it. He got up saying,"Damn it! It's salt water."

At night when all were asleep,Joe was tempted and slowly dragged himself to the bottle containing the last drops of water, took it up to his lips to drink when he heard a voice crying,"Water, water." It was Kennedy who was a pitiable sight. Joe gave him the bottle.

Just then Ferguson shouted,"Look there." When they looked they could see a cloud of sand advancing like a sea, fast. The doctor cried, "Simoon! Now we are going to live!"He then ran to the car and threw out all the sand which they had piled for ballast and the two companions also got in. he told Joe to throw out 50 pounds of his gold also which Joe quietly did. The ballon rose straight up and was carried full speed by the storm. By

3 o'clock, the storm abated and the wind stood still. They looked down and could see an oasis. "Water" they cried and brought the balloon down and all jumped down after taking their guns. Suddenly they heard a mighty roar and saw a huge lion in front of them.

Kennedy immediately sighted and shot the lion dead. He and Joe ran to the well and started lapping up the water from the spring happily. Kennedy filled a bottle to take to Ferguson but found that the way was blocked by a huge lioness. Kennedy aimed and fired but the lioness leaped back wounded. He put one more shot which killed her.

GOLD HAS TO BE THROWN OUT

"How strange our fortunes have been. Plenty after famine, Luxury after misery!" said Dick,"I nearly went mad." "Because of Joe we are alive now, Dick." said Kennedy, how we despaired for such a simple thing as water!"

"Water is very important, Joe,more important than food." said Ferguson.

"I can believe that. In emergencies a man

can eat anything. Even human meat. ”

“Yes,” said the doctor, “it is repulsive. So much so that when travellers told about savages eating raw flesh no one believed them. There is a story about a curious thing that happened to James Bruce.”

“Tell us, sir, we have enough time.” said Joe.

“James Bruce was a Scot who explored Abyssinia in search of the Nile between 1768 and 1772. He said that the East Africans ate raw meat. The public, on hearing this, rose against him. No one would listen to him and were sceptical about his reports. One day, in Edinburgh,in a drawing room, another Scot started the subject and accused Bruce of telling a lie. Bruce got up furious, went to the kitchen and came back with a raw steak,and said to the Scotsman “Sir, you have insulted me by saying I am lying. So to prove what I have reported, you will either eat this steak or face me in a duel. "

The Scotsman was so frightened that he ate the raw steak! James Bruce then said, "You can even say the statement is not true but now you cannot say it is impossible!"

"Good," said Joe, "if the Scotsman got indigestion it served him right! And if anyone doubts about our expedition,I will make him eat the balloon!"

"Are there Nyam Nyams here also?" asked Joe. "Yes, in the same type of climate they will have same habits. " Joe said, "It is natural. Savages do not have the same tastes as gentlemen. Anyway, they would have been happy to eat the Scotsman's steak and the Scotsman also!" They then prepared the fires and retired for the night.

Next day there was still no breeze and they were running short of provisions.

Would they die of starvation after nearly dying of thirst? But it was observed that the barometer was dropping which was a clear sign that the weather was changing. So they filled the food and water containers and got ready to leave. To retain the balance of the balloon Joe had to throw some gold. The doctor waited patiently for the weather to change,but in vain. But at 3 a.m. a huricane arose, so they took the balloon higher 200 feet.

1500 MILES COVERED

Joe was enjoying the scenery below. A lake surrounded by mountains. The valleys were fertile with many trees. there were elaeis with leaves 15 feet long, bombax from which cotton was being blown by the wind, pandanus or kewra, papaya and there were also some animals. Kennedy saw some elephants and said, "Oh! what beautiful elephants! Can we go hunting?" Not in this wind. Later. said Ferguson.

They could see wild ox, hippos,manatees and lots of rare species.

The doctor said, “We're lucky! We are going to connect the work of Barth and Speke. We have covered 25 degrees or 1500 miles.” 12 hours later, they could see the Alantika Mountains. At last they saw a river which Ferguson said was the Benue, a tributary of the Niger. At 5 p.m., after crossing Mount Mendif, they came down for hunting.

OUR FRIENDS ARE CONSIDERED SUPERNATURAL BEINGS

The next day, 11th May, the Victoria resumed her flight. As this was hostile country, Ferguson advised his companions to be alert. At about 9 a. m they came over Mosfeia town. Just then, a sheikh was entering with his troops.

His trumpeteers were blowing their trumpets loudly. Whwn they saw the balloon, all ran away but the sheikh stood with his musket cocked. The doctor came down within 50 yards and greeted him in Arabic. Hearing Ferguson,the sheikh got down and prostrated on the ground.

Ferguson said, "these natives take European for supernatural beings."

"What about the first Europeans who came here?"asked Joe,"who were they?"

The doctor replied, "Major Denham came to Mosfeia in 1822 and was robbed of all his belongings. He barely escaped with his life. Vogel crossed in 1836 but disappeared after he met Barth in 1854 and no one knows where he is now. Now we are heading towards Loggum district where Toole died. so you see we call this district 'the white man's grave".

The Shari was seen with canoes, 50 feet long, sailing. The wind was dropping now and they saw the town of Kernak.

"Can we go down nearer?" asked Joe. Ferguson replied,"Very easy!" He lowered the burner and they went down to 200 feet. It was a real town with a big market and rows of houses. There was also a slave market in the square.

When the populace saw the Victoria,there was a lot of shouting. The sheikh also came out of his house and gave a long speech which they could not make out but it was surely an order for them to go away. Then the sheikh lifted his musket to fire at the Victoria but Kennedy smashed it with a well-aimed shot. Then they rose up to escape.

BIRDS ATTACK—JOE JUMPS IN THE RIVER

They had a glimpse of Kuka, the capital of Bornu. There were a few mosques and houses. On one side the houses are big and on the other they are hovels. The wind changed direction and brought them back over Lake Tchad and they saw the small islands where pirates stayed. The savages could be seen ready with arrows and stones to attack them but they were too far off.

Joe turned to Kennedy and said, "Do you

see those 14 huge birds in front?"

Ferguson intervened and said," They are not birds but dangerous vultures."

The vultures were approaching the Victoria in a threatening mood. A few flew at speed and attacked the balloon. Even when Ferguson took it higher they also flew higher. Kennedy wanted to shoot at them but Ferguson disuaded him. Just then one of them darted straight at the balloon and Ferguson shouted,"Kennedy,shoot."

Kennedy fired and the bird fell down to the ground. Suddenly they heard a hiss and the balloon started to drop rapidly.

"We're finished" said Ferguson, "throw out the ballast." Though they threw out all the quartz,water and also the stores, the balloon was going down. "Throw something else." said Ferguson. There was nothing left to throw. Suddenly Joe jumped into the lake and the balloon rose again.

THE SEARCH FOR POOR JOE

The next day,the 13th May both woke up feeling very sad about Joe's loss. They found that they were on a small island surrounded by swamps.

Kennedy said, "Don't worry, Joe's a good swimmer. He will turn in time but we must make all efforts to find him.

Ferguson replied, "Pray to God you're right. Now first,we have to remove the torn outer balloon." Then, with great difficulty, they cut the damaged outer balloon into small pieces and removed each piece through the net.

Kennedy said, "I remember we fell near an island and Joe jumped off."

"Yes,but all these islands are inhabited by cut-throats and thieves. If Joe is captured by them what will be his fate?"

The doctor told Dick to go and shoot some meat as they had thrown all their provisions. They now had only 30 lbs of pemmican,some tea and coffee,and one and a half gallon of brandy.

Now he set about calculating the altered lifting force due the loss of the outer balloon and arrived at the sum of 2830 lbs to carry. So he compensated Joe's weight by extra ballast and the balloon was ready to be stable. By this time Kennedy returned with a good supply of geese,duck,teal and plover which he dressed and smoked and then stored. At night they had supper and slept. But each woke up several times looking out sadly for poor Joe.

In the morning,Ferguson said to Kennedy, "I have got a plan to find Joe." Dick said, "Tell me. I will follow you." Ferguson replied, "Now that we have a good wind to take us back over the lake we will go up so that he may see us and take courage even if he is a prisoner. Anyway, we will wait till we find him. "

Accordingly, at 7 a. m, they weighed anchor and rose and kept level between 200 and 500 feet heading towards the lake at 20 mph. searching all over the ground for Joe.

By 2.30 o'clock they passed the village Tangalia. As a gale started in the morning, they had to leave but promised to return for Joe.

A CARVAN IS BURIED IN THE SAND

"Poor Joe!" said the doctor, "he was so kind-hearted and brave. He even threw the gold out though it meant so much to him. Even if we have to abandon the Victoria we will return for him to Lake Tchad on foot and ask the Sultan to help us.

The Victoria now passed the Tibbus and reached the desert area completely bare of plants or trees. They were wondering whether they would have to cross the Sahara like this when they saw a caravan of Arabs struggling in the middle of a whirlwind and sand storm. Soon all the horses and humans were buried under the sand! The Victoria was being tossed about violently and going backwards.

"The wind is taking us back to the places we wanted," said the doctor, "towards south where we will come across the towns of Bornu, Wuddie or Kuka where I will stop."

JOE HAILS THE VICTORIA IN VAIN

Let's see what happened to Joe.

When he jumped in the lake and looked up, he could see the Victoria going up and he said to himself, "A good thing I jumped out. One person sacrified to save two! That's simple mathematics. "He had jumped in the centre of the lake surrounded by fierce tribes but he was not afraid. He got rid of his heavier clothing and started swimming for the bank. As he approached the bank he was nervous of the fierce crocodiles. A little later, he got the sickly smell of musk and felt the presence of a crocodile so he dived and actually scraped a crocodile and started swimming more fast. He heard a sound behind him and was seized by the arm and later by the waist. He thought, "This is my end!" but he saw that he was held by two negroes. Had he fallen from the frying pan into the fire?

They brought him to the bank where a huge crowd gathered and started shouting and touching his garments. They all prostrated before him and started giving him milk and rice mixed with honey thinking him a god. he enjoyed the meal and attention. In the evening the witch doctors took him to a hut surrounded by talismans which were bones! There was a lot of singing and dancing and sound of drums outside the hut.

He wondered how long this adoration would last. would it end in them eating him?"

Thinking thus, he fell asleep. In the middle of the night,he felt some dampness and woke up to find that the place was filling with water. He broke the wall with one powerful blow and found that the island had got covered by the waters of Lake Tchad. This was a common phenomenon in these parts. Joe started swimming and saw an empty boat hollowed out of a log and climbed into it and started drifting. He looked at the North Star and saw with satisfaction that he was drifting towards the northern shore of the lake. At two in the morning he saw a tree and slept in its branches. When he woke up in the morning, to his horror he saw that the tree was full of snakes! He quickly jumped down.

Luckily he stopped at once and hid from a band of savages. Looking up, he saw the Victoria coming back but he could not call out or show himself. He saw it sail away and tears came to his eyes, not for himself but out of gratitude that his friends were saved!

In despair he cried, "Master! Sir! Help!" But his cry died away into the night!

JOE IS SPOTTED—AND SAVED

Kennedy suddenly shouted from his post, "I can see a cloud of sand down below. It looks like a band of men or animals. Sometimes it looks like horsemen. "

After a pause he said, "Yes. It is horsemen! Look." The doctor looked and said "Yes. It is that." While watching, some horsemen broke away from the group. "The're Arabs. Their chief is in the lead." Kennedy, watching said.

"Whatever it is we are safe. We can rise anytime." said Ferguson. Kennedy now said,"It is a manhunt. And that is not the chief but their quarry."

"Dont lose sight of them." the doctor told him. They were gaining on the Arabs and Suddenly Kennedy shouted,"Samuel! Samuel! That's Joe they're chasing! He's on horseback and he cannot see us."

"He will," Ferguson said,"in 10 minutes we will lower and in fifteen we will be over him. " and he lowered the flame.

Suddenly Joe's horse gave out and fell but Joe caught hold of an Arab and threw him down and jumped on his horse and waving to the Victoria which he had seen by now, he galloped following the same course.

They brought the balloon lower and threw out a rope which Joe caught and climbed into the car and was saved.

ON THEIR WAY TO TIMBUKTU

"We were worried about you, Joe," said Ferguson. Joe said, "I was also worried about you. You gave me a fright. I will cook this goose shot by Mr. Kennedy and then tell you my story." The bird was cooked and after a hearty meal and some tea and brandy, Joe told his story.

"I kept walking when I saw some horses tethered. I took one and rode away. I went on and on through towns and fields and pallisades till like a fool I rode into an Arab camp. Now I was the quarry. I knew that you would find me. You know the rest, how you saved me." Then the doctor said he would take them to Timbuktu.

THEY REACH TIMBUKTU

On 17 May they replenished their water stock and left. On Sunday morning they passed some crows and vultures. They had reached 16 deg. N long. 4 deg. 55 min. E The doctor said,"This inner ballon is not so good. It is losing gas so I am expanding the gas to keep us up. There is no remedy so we will have to stop halting at night. They saw a long string of camels with lots of women and young children travelling. Joe asked how they managed to find their way without any roads or compasses through the desert. The doctor replied that Arabs were very good sign readers and noticed each bush and stone on the route.

At noon they passed over the town of Gao, where, the doctor said, Barth crossed the Niger while returning from Timbuktu. He said,"This area has been the scene of many sacrifices by former explorers like Saugnier, Brisson, Adam, Riley,Mungo Park and scores of others. Richard Lander faced a lot of hardships in two trips and during his 3rd expedition he was murdered. So you see, friends, brave acts are often rewarded with death. Soon they crossed tributaries of the Niger and were above the large port tom of Timbuktu with its narrow streets and small houses, mosques and fort.

The balloon was heading towards the southwest which worried Ferguson as they would go towards South Africa where the barbarians lived. Suddenly Joe cried, "Rain! I see a thick cloud." Ferguson looked through his glass and said, "No, it's a great swarm of locusts. They settled on a forest and in no time all the trees and bushes were bare! They were now going towards the Senegal River.

JOE SAVES THEM ALL

On the 27th May morning the Victoria showed signs of dropping gradually which the doctor attributed to the leaking of gas through the heat-softened gutta percha. The doctor said, “We cannot prevent it so we must lighten her by throwing out whatever we can spare.” Then they threw the tent. The balloon rose for a short time then again started going down. Kennedy suggested going down and repairing the balloon but the doctor said there were too many wild animals and dangerous tribes there who would kill them if they captured them.

"We are not far from the river but we may not get accross because there are some mountains to cross."

As he said this, the mountains came in sight. As they were higher than the Victoria, they threw out the water, then the containers, still the height was not enough and the balloon was heading for the rocks. "Throw out all the meat and keep only the pemmican, Joe." said Ferguson. Still not enough.

The doctor said, "Be ready to sacrifice your guns, Dick." "My guns!" cried Dick. "I would not ask unless it was absolutely necessary. "Ferguson said. Joe threw out some blankets and Kennedy threw some bags of powder and shot.

"Kennedy! Throw out your guns!"shouted Ferguson. "Wait!" shouted Joe and jumped out of the balloon. "He's gone!" wailed Ferguson. Immediately the balloon rose up and just scraped the top of the mountain!

"It's over! Its crossed!" said a well-loved voice and Joe, who had jumped to reduce the load of his weight and run along with it across the crest, climbed into the car "Splendid job, Joe,"said the doctor, "you saved us twice!"

"I did it to save Mr. Kennedy's guns. They saved my life from the Arabs. I always pay my debts. Now we are quits!" said Joe.

As night came Ferguson decided to anchor as he wanted to carry out a plan. Soon the anchors were out and the Victoria set down.

ATTACKED BY BANDITS

In the morning when Ferguson took a reckoning,he found that they were hardly 25 miles from the Senegal. He told them that since there were no bridges or boats they had to cross by the balloon, so they had to lighten the balloon to the limit.

"We will get rid of the burner, battery and spiral which weigh 900 lbs. We have gas enough to carry the three of us and the anchors. It was a major job to dismantle the spiral, mixing chamber and burner from the balloon without harming the balloon. But Kennedy's strength and Joe's agility did the job.

Kennedy kept dozing now and then and was awake with difficulty. Finally he fell asleep. Suddenly he woke up hearing a crackling sound and saw flames. He shouted "Fire! Fire!" The two companions got up and cut the anchor rope and rose just as the dangerous Talibas, bandits of Al Hadji came yelling.

THEY SUCCEED BUT THE VICTORIA DIES

One Taliba fired a shot and Kennedy returned the fire and one horseman dropped dead. The balloon was now at ground level and started going up and down with the bandits chasing. Ferguson told Joe, "We must rise or we are lost! Drop the pemmican, reserves of brandy and all the instruments!" Joe threw everything out and the balloon used to rise and fall after some time. "Throw the two guns. " Kennedy did so after firing four shots which dropped 4 horsemen. The Victoria rose again and bounced like a ball.

The balloon seemed to be getting tired. The doctor suddenly cried out, "Throw out the car and hang on to the net. That weighs 150 lbs." As soon as they did so, the balloon sprang up 300 feet. The Victoria found a favourable breeze and went fast leaving the bandits behind and cleared a hill. They could see the Senegal river now!

"Fifteen minutes more and we're saved!" said Kennedy. But unfortunately the Victoria came down and the net got caught in the tree branches and she came down only 100 feet from the river. The bandits were close now and there seemed no hope for the three.

Suddenly Ferguson shouted, "All is not lost yet! Only 15 minutes more. Collect all the dried grass. We will fly on hot air as there is no gas left. " So they collected lots of hay and lit it under the balloon. At this time the Talibas were only 2 miles behind them shouting and galloping.

The fire burned and slowly the balloon filled and started jerking. The three hung on to the net as she rose to 800 feet and approached the river and 10 minutes later were slowly drawn to the other bank. But the balloon was now on fire.

A group of French soldiers were looking as the balloon fell in the river and the three occupants swam to shore sadly because the Victoria was lost.

CONCLUSION

The French-men were an expedition sent by the Governor of Senegal to establish a station at Guina Falls. There were applauding and congratulations for our three friends all over! Ferguson requested the officers to witness and sign a paper as proof of their landing :

Guina Falls, 24th May 1862

"We, the undersigned, declare that we

witnessed the arrival of Dr. Ferguson and his companions, Richard Kennedy and Joseph Wilson, clinging to the net of a balloon which fell a few yards from us into the river and was dragged away over the Guina Falls. In confirmation of this, we sign the aforementioned report.

SAMUEL FERGUSON, RICHARD KENNEDY, JOSEPH WILSON DUFRAISE, Lieut. d'Infanterie de marine RODAMEL, enseigne de vaisseau DUFAYS, sergent FLIPPEAU MAYOR, pelissier LORIS, RASCAGNET, GUILLON, LEBEL, soldats

Thus ended the successful voyage of Dr. Ferguson and his brave companions. After felicitations and receptions at Medina,and St. Louis they were in London on 25th June.

All the papers were full of praise for them and their feat. The Royal Geographic Society honoured them with a gold medal for the most noteworthy exploration of the year 1862.

Ferguson left for Edinburgh with his famous carbine.